Moving a Puddle

ISBN: 1-4116-4868-4

First printing September 2005, Sandra Dodd, Albuquerque
Second printing August 2006, Sandra Dodd, Albuquerque

Printed in the U.S.A.

Moving a Puddle

and other essays

by Sandra Dodd

INTRODUCTION

These essays and little riffs were published between 1992 and 2005, during which time my firstborn son went from six to nineteen years of age. In earlier writings I used terminology I have long since abandoned, but I notice that in the first one I did put quotation marks around "education" because even when Kirby was first-grade age, I knew the idea of "education" was a mire. Better to start clean with the simplest ideas, and so gradually I let go of more and more schooly-words.

The overall theme is how learning, parenting and everyday life can be in the absence of school, viewed from different vantage points over a dozen years. I hope there are ideas to help every reader, whether homeschooler or not, whether unschooler or not. Any parent or anyone who loves learning for fun should find something to help thoughts form and swirl.

Knowing I've left a few out, I tried to indicate prior publication, as these essays have all been published at least once. I was compiling credits and dates from paper copies of newsletters and magazine I've collected, and a few were unreceived or unfiled. Articles have been published in international magazines, and in local/regional publications in the U.S., Canada, New Zealand, Australia and France. "Public School on your Own Terms" was translated into Japanese when Linda Dobson's book in which it appeared was translated some years ago. "Playing" will appear in a book in France within the next few months, and as I was doing final edit I received a request for permission to translate that essay into Italian. People say the water's all the same, so something that starts in a puddle in New Mexico can end up being a fluff of a cloud in Italy or France. It's all connected.

Sandra Dodd

CONTENTS

Photos by Sandra Dodd, except:

> page 22 by Kirby Dodd
> page 28 by either Kris or Cabral Williams
> page 40 by Mary Lou Adams
>   (except the VW)
> page 45 by Holly Dodd
> page 56 by Annaliese Mayette
> page 94 by Marty Dodd (I think)
> page 98 by Tamarind King
> page 152 ff. by Irene Adams

Scanner art (puzzle and pattern blocks) by Sandra and Holly Dodd

Structure

*"How do I structure our days
and how do I structure our learning time?"*

I felt moved to suggest an answer to the question about how to structure a day of child-directed learning. I think it should be "Woke up, got dressed, ate, played, ate, played, etc." In other words, I don't think there should or can be any "days off" from child-centered "education."

If this seems wrong, try this experiment: Keep your child from learning anything for a few days. Make sure that from the first waking moment there is nothing learned, no new material, no original thoughts to ponder, etc. The only problem is that you would have to keep the children from playing, talking, reading, cleaning or repairing anything, etc.

We have a new neighbor who attends private school. On the way home one day he wanted to get an invitation to come back to play the next day, and he phrased it this way: "Does Kirby have homeschool tomorrow?" (My less memorable answer was "homeschool is just sort of whenever." Had I known I would be writing this I would have tried to be more profound.) The answer was YES! but that might have made my neighbor feel unwelcome. Little does he suspect that he is a guest instructor at our 365-day-per-year homeschool!

> (This was part of the "Dear Susanna" column in the September 1992 issue of *The Connection*, the newsletter of *New Mexico Family Educators*. Kirby was six years old. The neighbor was seven.)

Kirby and Marty trying out a new trashcan.

February 27, 1995
I wrote this to a small e-mail loop of some of the best of those writing about homeschooling on AOL in that season. One of them sent this to Home Education Magazine's letters section, where it was published. I've left it in its original breathless one-paragraph format, lifted straight from the original e-mail.

Gilligan's Island

When I used to watch Gilligan's Island in 4:00 re-runs after school every day, I would wonder whose idea it was for the plot, how many writers there were, how they decided who could come and visit, what device they would use to prevent the visitor from rescuing them, how they must plan in advance not to have too-similar plots near each other, and the re-runs must be kept in that same order too. I wondered about them changing the theme song—at first it had said, "the movie star, and the rest," but in later seasons it said, "the movie star, the professor and Mary Ann," and I wondered whether they had re-sung the whole thing or just spliced in that line, because it sounded the same as it had before. And had they done it because the actors complained? Their agents complained? I wondered whether the pedal-powered washing machine (or whatever it was) really worked by the pedals, or whether it was just secretly plugged in, and if so, where did the wires run? I wondered if much of it was on indoor sets. How deep was that water? (As an adult, I saw what's left of the set at Universal Studios. Cool! Outside! Actual little lake.) When I would see a show the second time, I'd look around for things I had missed the first time. I would re-write lines in my mind, things that could have been funnier, or sounded more in character for that person. I'd wonder who knew more about hammock making, the captain or the professor? Maybe Ginger or Mary Ann knew macramé. When there was a show that didn't have one of the actors in, I'd wonder whether he was sick or on vacation or what? And if an actor misses the filming of a sitcom, does he still get paid? I wondered about them having to keep their hair the same for years, and which of them might be wearing wigs. Where were they supposed to be getting nail polish and lipstick? Hair spray? I wondered if the professor was a physics professor or engineering, or what, and whether he would lose his job at the university. I wondered about that Mr. Magoo voice on Thurston Howell. I wondered about Amelia Earhart. I wondered about the soundtrack music. Did they just have little themes they pushed a button on during final edit, or was each show done separately? I wondered if the fruit was real or props. I wondered about cameras—where were they? Did they have to sweep the dirt between takes? I wondered if the guy who played the lost WWII pilot was really Japanese. I could think more during an episode of Gilligan's Island than most other people I knew could think in a whole week. I didn't bother to ask my parents any of the questions. They would have thought it was stupid to be thinking them. So to all outside appearances (except to my cousin, Nada, who was my age) I was just zoning out, involved in the plot of another 25 minutes of Gilligan's Island. That wasn't true at all.

Marty as a pirate and
Kirby as a cowboy with Ninja Turtle boots

You Could Grow Up to be President!

"You could grow up to be President." I don't know how many times I heard that in school and I suppose it's true. Some people have, and they were all kids once, but what are the odds? I got to thinking about the number of people who thought they *might* want to be president never made it, and how they felt about that. I didn't feel like interviewing a sufficient number of people to make a scientific sample, so the article's not about that.

I thought I would find out what percentage of the people born in a particular year *had* become president, so I chose 1900. I figured it would be a simple problem—find out how many eligible Americans were born, and how many became president! There were problems. First, I found that nobody born in 1900 had become president. Then I couldn't find out how many people were born! The problem was, four states (including my own) weren't even part of the U.S. yet. I tried several sources to get birth figures for the entire eligible U.S.; no go. Alaska, Hawaii, Arizona and New Mexico? Well the problem is, how many of them lived to the age of 35? And do we count women, who still today don't have a snowball's chance in Kilauea of becoming president? So I thought back; what's realistic? The depression and the flu epidemic were after 1900, as was WWI, and those who lived through all that ripened for the presidential elections in 1948. In 1948 nobody would've considered anyone who was Black or Hispanic, Asian or German. Jewish? Yeah. Maybe *next* century. How many were left? Who knows? I got tired of the question.

From 1891 to 1907, sixteen full years, not a single future president was born. So it's possible that nobody born from 1991 to 2007 will be president either. And listen—if one of them IS president, why would you want it to be one of *your* kids? Why would you wish a full-year campaign and four years of round-the-clock worry and international responsibility on a child of yours? Why would you want your child to risk being vice president and having to attend the funerals of strangers all over the world where he might inadvertently insult an entire culture by some everyday hand gesture that means "OK" here but something horribly scatological there? Not only that, it would be on international TV!

You should think of these things before you give your children any big ideas about being president.

Most people say they wish they could keep their children young a little longer. I've never met many who would willingly put their kids in an aging-chamber (well, except around the time they're fourteen... never mind that now). Look at photos of Jimmy Carter before and after, or of Clinton. People go in young or middle-aged and come out *old*. If I wanted my kids to age quickly I'd just buy them cigarettes (and tell them to smoke somewhere besides at *my* house). No, I want my kids to last a while, and to age no more quickly than necessary.

So what *is* a worthy goal for us to set for our children? I heard about a family with a chart on the wall culminating in a scholarship to Notre Dame. It worked backwards into the present, so that if the child met all the lower-level goals, the scholarship was a done deal. The kid was only nine years old or so, and the parents had made the chart themselves, but hey! People need GOALS!! (In our collective defense, these people weren't homeschooling.) What are their odds of failure? A scholarship to Harvard would be a failure.

Here are my goals for my children: I want them to learn something every day. I want them to greet the morning with joy. I want them to see strangers as potential friends. I want their lives to be adventures without a map, where there are innumerable destinations, and unlimited opportunities for "success." I want their definition of success to include things they can see all around them, not just in Washington, not just at medical conventions, or the Olympics. I want them to wake up, look out the window, and be glad of the view. I want them to be content with their choices and their abilities. I want them to be realistic about goals and philosophical about failure. I want them to be happy.

The really good thing about happiness is that it's portable. It's cheap. It doesn't need a safety deposit box or an inheritance. You can give the same amount to all your kids, and they don't have to wait until they're 18 to claim and use it! Think about that. They can have it right now, and start using it, without taking yours away from you.

Do kids need to have their own room to store their happiness in? No. Do kids need to wait nine weeks to get a report card that says they're doing well in happiness? No. Will working really hard now store up happiness they can use later? That's the going theory, the one we were raised on, but I no longer believe it.

If my children wake up in Albuquerque, happy to be who and where they are, I hope they can maintain that feeling every day until they wake up in the middle of the next century and look out—I don't care what they're looking at, whether it's the Alps, the Rio Grande, the back of their own filling station or the White House lawn—and they're still happy to be who and where they are. Who could ask for more than happiness? Don't wait. Get it today and give it away.

Home Education Magazine, May/June 1996

6

Taking Advantage of Mr. Toad

Ta-daa!!!! Something new. I am Sandra Dodd, writing to you from Albuquerque, New Mexico, at Mary Kate's request. When my family traveled to Southern California for the Home=Education Conference in April, my online penpal, Pam, took us to Ralph B. Clark Regional Park to meet some of the local homeschooling families. It was great. Marty, who's seven, was happy to be a flying monkey for a day. My other two children are Kirby, who will be ten this summer, and Holly, our only girl, who's four. I was glad for my husband, Keith, to get to hang around in a leisurely fashion with other homeschoolers. When we're home he misses the play days because he's loyally and selflessly at work. What a guy.

Of course, we went to Disneyland, and although I resisted, we rode Mr. Toad's Wild Ride. I had been told by someone in line with us (even the lines are educational at Disneyland) that the ride had been expanded and spruced up. That made me think different thoughts as I rode the little car through Toadhall, the English countryside, and on into Hell.

I don't suppose I am the only person with this particular problem: there are things in my own area that my nine-year-old son has never seen. I've been to Bandelier National Monument eight or ten times in my life. Being in "been there, done that" mode, I have never taken my own children. I was grown and married before I saw Carlsbad Caverns, six hours from here. It's not that I had never been to Carlsbad— we had relatives there! My parents met and courted in Carlsbad. I had been to the town of Carlsbad several times, but all my relatives had "been there, done that." My grandfather had worked on the park when it was new. Nobody wanted to take me out to the caverns.

You'd think that would have "taught me a lesson," but never, all last summer, did I take my children to the local amusement park or water park here in town. I get lazy about familiar things. In California, thanks to five-day passes and a close hotel, I went to Disneyland four times in five days. My kids and husband went *eight* times in five days. I bet some of the families reading this haven't been for a year or two.

On the way to Disneyland Monday, our last day, I asked the kids who they thought had fixed up Mr. Toad's Wild Ride, who had worked on it. "Walt Disney," Marty said. Nope, he's dead. A lot of people worked on it. What kinds of people? They understood the question then and started reeling off the names of professions (with Keith's help, and mine)—artists/designers, carpenters, electricians, safety engineers, metalworkers (welders? pipefitters?), plumbers (for heat/air conditioning), musicians? recording engineers? painters (both of the serviceable house-painting sort, and graphic artists). No doubt there were more.

We went in and rode the ride again. They saw it differently. I noticed details I hadn't seen earlier. We could have made an entire "study" of Mr. Toad's Wild Ride, and it's not even one of the highlights of Disneyland!

That little conversation lasted less than five minutes. In educational terms it would have qualified as analytical reasoning, life skills, and career awareness (or whatever it is being called this year). They learned more from answering one question about something they were already thinking about than they could have learned from a detailed unit study on *The Wind and the Willows* and its adaptation as a theme-park ride. If I had told them, "Of all the rides here, *this* is the one I will turn to an educational purpose," I would have been giving them a very odd message.

The experiences my children gained in a marathon Disneyland weekend will never be fully analyzed. I regularly trot out my oldest memories and reexamine them in light of new data or ideas. Sometimes an incident has to be jazzy or flashy to stick in memory, sometimes it just has to have some pre-existing memory to connect to, or have an element of sound, smell, sight, taste or emotion that will earn it a special place in one's personal history. Memories are never lacking in import. Things with no import are not remembered well at all. Your children's memories are the elements of which their selves are made—their personality, store of knowledge, bag of tricks, personal resources, all reside in memory and their ability to mentally manipulate facts and ideas.

There are millions of American children who will never see Disneyland, La Brea Tarpits or the Pacific Ocean. There are millions more whose parents will never point out to them the wonders of such things, the visions and handiwork of the humans who make them safely and cleanly accessible to us, and what similar things they might want to do during their own lifetimes. Why should any homeschooling families be among them? We have time and reason to provide our children with enriching experiences.

I'm taking my children to Bandelier before the end of May to see the cliff dwellings and the museum. I'll remind them that it was from the work of real human beings who built trails, the ladders up to the cliffs, the visitor center and a road up the canyon that we are able to see these ancient homes. Because of the work of archeologists we can see pottery and tools that were found beneath the floor of the canyon. Because of the careful labor of student workers, we can see the old pueblo, its rooms and its kivas in partially excavated form.

There are wonderful things in your area. Even if you've seen them over and over, please take advantage of their nearness to fill your children's heads with ideas, images, questions and theories. I will be doing the same thing, here in New Mexico, with my own family.

CHN *Network News* (California), June/July 1996

Public School on Your Own Terms

There are people who are solidly homeschoolers and happy to be so. There are others who are wholly involved in and supportive of the public schools their kids attend. Then there are those with a foot in each world. Using my sister as a test case, I made a radical recommendation that she chose to implement, and it turned out well. Since then I've given this advice several times and haven't been sued (yet). Nobody's even asked for a refund!

Here is the way my sister overcame her school codependency: She divorced herself emotionally and politically from the public school.

I have one sister, three years younger than I am. I was a star pupil, junior honor society member, extracurricular queen, member of the band, all-state chorus... Younger sisters in the readership are already sympathizing with my B-student sister. She went out with the younger brothers of my boyfriends a couple of times. She could not get out of my shadow. She dropped out of high school not long before I became a teacher. I was invested in the system. She had rejected it.

Years passed, and we each had three children. While I opted not to send mine to school at all, my sister was a "room mother" and gifted-program advisory board member, and she chaperoned field trips. Her older boy wrote at the age of five. Mine didn't *read* until he was eight. The evidence that she was right and I was wrong was increasing, which must have been a great feeling for her. (It happens more and more as the years go by, and I don't mind at all.)

Another thing was increasing, though. From once a month, to once a week, to every other day, my sister called and complained about something at school, and I would play devil's advocate, or give her considerations the teacher had that my sister might not have known. At first I was sympathetic. Then I was apathetic. After a while I got irritated, and one day I cut her off in advance of the tale of woe, saying, "You already know what I'm going to say. You don't *have* to send them to school."

It was springtime. She decided to spend the summer preparing them for the idea of staying home if they wanted to, but meanwhile she needed a way for their being in school not to ruin *her* life. I recommended that she just detach. She was no longer going to enable the teachers to torment her children. She quit forcing them to do homework. She quit even considering punishing them for bad grades or rewarding them for good grades. Their grades were theirs, and not a reflection on the family, and not an indicator of learning. They were just grades, a contest, a competition like who sold the most candy bars, only my sister quit buying the candy bars, as it were. She quit helping with the homework.

The year after that, her daughter who is the oldest of three stayed home instead of going to 4th grade. The boys went to school. When they felt ill they were allowed

9

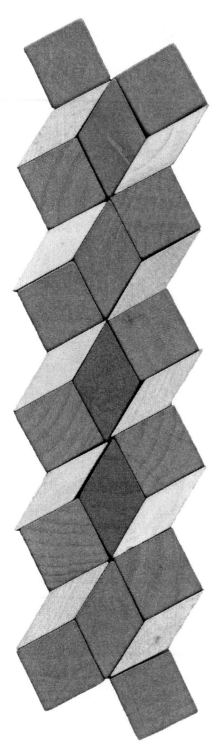

to stay home without having to have fever or puke to earn the privilege. They became more honest. Sometimes they just said, "I don't want to go to school today." She would say, "You don't have to then. I wish you just would never go again." So their first reward was renewed and increased honesty. (When I called my sister to read this to her for verification, she asked me to add that if she had it to do over she wouldn't be so honest as to announce to the principal, "School is optional at our house." She advises you to make assorted excuses like the other parents do.)

The second year the daughter went back because she had missed her friends. The dynamics of that school year, though, were phenomenal. Neither my sister nor I had foreseen the extent to which this detachment would free the entire family, and hadn't considered the effect on the relationship between the children and their teachers. No longer were these children in school against their will, their parents having submitted them to a lock-up situation. On one hand they had teachers who wanted them to stay in school. On the other hand they had parents who wanted them to stay home. How much more "wanted" could they feel? Each moment they were in school they were aware, and the teacher was aware, that they were there because they, the children, *wanted* to be there! These factors changed the way the kids responded to assignments, to interpersonal problems, and to threats from the teacher (which have little power without the backing of the parents.)

In late winter, the daughter contracted a staph pneumonia and was in a hospital ninety miles from home for a couple of weeks. After that she didn't want to return to school (and her recovery was better served by staying home, too). One of her brothers left school at that time as well, and next year all three plan to stay home. When school starts and they don't go, how different it will be for them than it is in those families in which the children pine for school but their parents forbid them to go.

There are different reasons for homeschooling. School might not be an option at all in a family in which religious or social considerations take precedence. In families in which student-directed learning is the primary focus, children taking control of their own learning by deciding whether to pursue it at home or at school can be liberating for all involved, and educational in the extreme for their teachers.

Although the ideal might be children who have never gone to school a day in their lives, reality isn't always ideal. If your children press you to let them go to school, this detachment option might be a way for you to have your cake and eat it too. The philosophies of choice, freedom, child-led learning, "bliss-led learning," and personal responsibility can be honored and spread to new audiences by parents treating children as humans with rights and responsibilities whether they are sixteen, twelve, or eight years old.

CHN Network News (California), August/September 1996
Linda Dobson's *Homeschool Book of Answers,* 1998
(which has been translated into Japanese)

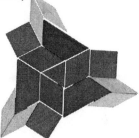

[something I wrote later to a mom:]

I think it will make a difference to his view of school as soon as you say with feeling and truth, "You can come home anytime you want to."

I would tell his teachers, too, that you would prefer to homeschool him, but that he is choosing to stay there for the time being. It might make them think twice about being butts to him.

The next time school is horribly unreasonable, he can walk dramatically!

Every moment that he knows that is an empowered moment, and every dealing he has with a teacher or a kid is not the dealing of a powerless child who is there against his will, but of a person with an open door behind him.

—Sandra

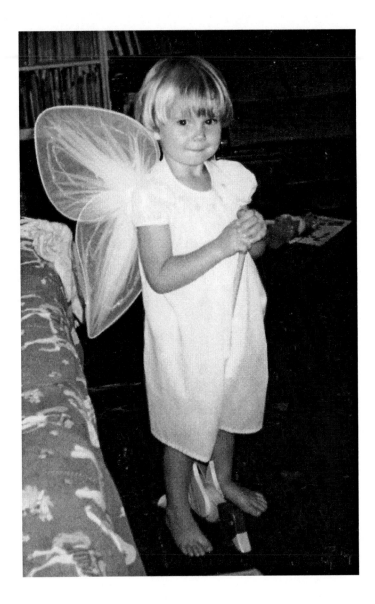

Rejecting a Pre-Packaged Life

How many things do you do because you're supposed to, because your relatives and neighbors expect it, because it's easy and you don't have to think about it? How many of those things are taking you and your kids in a positive and healthy direction?

"Changing paradigms" is an option! If you're operating on one plane, with one set of rules and expectations, it is possible and often advisable, to shift and see things differently. It's just thinking. It won't hurt you.

Is school the center of children's lives? Should it be?

Is the only acceptable goal of adult life having the most expensive house and furniture credit will buy?

It doesn't take much of a shift to consider house and education secondary instead of primary. What might be primary then? Health? Joy? Togetherness and love?

Part of the pre-packaged life Americans are issued is the idea that happiness comes after college, after home ownership, after the new car. The stick that holds that carrot will not bend. If happiness depends on performance and acquisition, how long will it last? How long is your car the newest on your street before unhappiness returns?

Here's a little paradigm shift for you to practice on. Perhaps happiness shouldn't be the primary goal. Try joy. Try the idea that it might be enJOYable to cook, to set the table, to see your family, rather than the idea that you'll be happy after dinner's done and cleaned up. My guess is that such happiness might last a couple of seconds before you look around and see something else between you and happiness. Joy, though, can be ongoing, and can be felt before, during and after the meeting of goals.

Enjoyment—that word itself is hardly used. Enjoyment is seen nearly as a sin for some people. "You're not here to have fun, you're here to work." Why can't work bring joy? Any tiny moment can be enjoyed: the feel of warm running water when you wash your hands; light and shadow on the floor; pictures in the clouds; the feel of an old book. If you see an old friend that can bring pure, tingly joy for which there are no words.

If you practice noticing and experiencing joy, if you take a second out of each hour to find joy, your life improves with each remembrance of your new primary goal. You don't need someone else to give you permission, or to decide whether or not what you thought gave you joy was an acceptable source of enjoyment.

Can learning be fun? If it's not fun, it won't stick. Can laundry be fun? If you

13

have to do laundry and you choose *not* to enjoy it, an hour or more of your precious time on earth will be wasted. Can looking at your child bring you joy even when he needs a bath and has lost a shoe and hasn't lived up to some expectation that only exists in your mind? If not, a paradigm shift could help you both.

Your life is yours, and it is being lived even as you read this. Do not wait for approval. Do not wait for instructions, or for a proctor to say "Open your lifebook now and write." Have all the joy you want, and help your children, neighbors and relatives find some too. Joy doesn't cost anything but some reusable thought and awareness. Tell your kids it's recyclable. They'll love that!

Enchanted Families (Premier Issue), Fall 1997
Kootenay Home Educators, Winter '98
S.I.G.H.T., Fall 2001
SoHome Bulletin, March 2002

(Those publications were/are local to, respectively, Albuquerque, New Mexico; Kootenay, British Columbia; southern Idaho and Humboldt County, California.)

All Kinds of Homeschooling

When the deadline was upon me and I was pacing around, my son Kirby said, "Why don't you write about 'What I Did on My Vacation in Timbuktu' and then make it up from there?" Well, I could write about what we did on vacation, but since we homeschool the same way all year and the kids learn more out of town than in, there is no vacation. We went to Ontario, anyway, not Timbuktu.

I kept pacing and whimpering.

"Write it like *Lone Wolf*," he said. "If you want to learn about math, go to page 132. If you want to learn about science, turn to page 53."

Now *there* is an idea—education as a Choose-Your-Own-Adventure book. Now he's onto something. I mean now I'm writing.

There are many ways to homeschool. Surprisingly (*not*) homeschoolers sometimes look askance at styles which are not their own. Extremists at both ends have complained that they hate to be tarred with the same brush as [fill in the blank with "Other"].

Some homeschoolers are very structured. They do school-style work, with subjects, units, tests, grades, on a schedule with vacations (in Timbuktu, perhaps, but without schoolwork when they get there). They fear to hear, "Oh, so you're homeschooling; you just let your kids do whatever they want?"

Some homeschoolers structure their lives on the open classroom models used in the early 1970's. They were big in many New Mexico school districts, so some of you reading this might have taught in one, or attended one. This is a structure based on removal of the traditional structure, on interest-based learning, on discovery learning. People enamored of this approach fear to hear, "Oh, you're a homeschooler. So you don't let your children play outside the house with other children?" or "So, call me when your lessons are over."

I'm an unschooler. Lessons are never over. On the other hand, lessons never really begin. Children's questions are answered and an atmosphere of learning is created so that questions are constant and answers are never far away.

When people ask a structured family how much time it takes to homeschool the response usually ranges from three to six hours a day (much more than kids actually spend learning/working in classrooms in school). When you ask an unschooling family how much time it takes to homeschool, first there's a pause. I've heard, in rapid succession in groups of unschoolers, "None" and "All of it." Their range is it takes from zero hours a day to 24 hours a day.

When learning is recognized in the fabric of life and encouraged, when families make their decisions based on what leads to more interesting and educational ends, children learn without effort, often without even knowing it, and parents learn along with them.

Many homeschoolers fall somewhere between structured and seamless-life learners. There are families whose children attend school whose houses are learning labs, museums and libraries all rolled into one. Enriching our lives for the benefit of our children isn't just for homeschoolers. Small changes in parental attitude are sometimes all it takes.

Learning isn't in fancy books or computer games, it all happens in the ideas children have, in the trivial facts they fit together to come up with their view of the world—past, present and future. You don't need a lesson or a unit to show a child what's wonderful about wood grain, ice crystals on the windshield, or birdsongs. Five seconds worth of pointing and saying "Look, these trees were not native to North America" might possibly lead to an hour-long discussion, or a lifelong fascination. Bringing something interesting home, browsing in an antique shop, listening to new music on instruments you've never heard—all those build neural pathways and give you a chance to be together in a special place.

No matter how your children learn, take a few more opportunities to share wonder and discovery with them. It will enrich you all.

Enchanted Families, February/March 1998

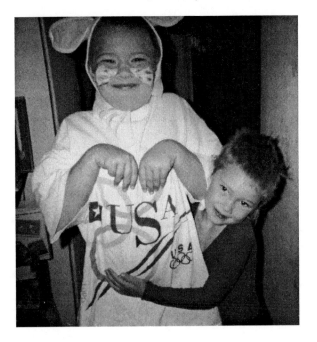

Holly and the Easter Marty

What you can do with your dictionary and encyclopedia...

A Radical Thought

Never tell a child "Go look it up." Parents, teachers, friends and countrymen, how would you like it?

When a child wants to know why flowers have a scent, they want someone to say "To attract bees" not *"Go look it up."*

"Go look it up" tends to mean "I don't know" or "I know but I'm not going to tell you." What's the advantage of that?

Either a child will opt *not* to look it up (and the trust in the parent will erode a little) or he will, under duress, perform this task, which might be difficult for him, or might take so long that he doesn't care anymore (and the trust in the parent will erode a little).

I'm *not* saying to discourage kids from looking things up. I never said not to show kids how to look things up. I mean don't treat it like something parents won't do, parents don't have to do, but that kids do, or that kids have to do, because they are powerless kids.

Encyclopedias should be alluring, not forbidding. Dictionaries should be a playland, not a dark, scary place you dart into for one thing and slam shut behind you. If you believe they *are* fun, you should look things up in front of your children, often, and with enthusiasm. That will teach them how to use reference materials, and will make them want to do so, because they will see it as something useful and enjoyable that adults do. If you believe dictionaries and encyclopedias *are* dark, scary and forbidding, why on *earth* would you send your children there?

Enchanted Families, February/March 1998
(It was filler; I had a full article elsewhere in that issue.)

Marty in armor, with six-shooter and boots

Moving a Puddle

I've long been an advocate of natural learning and unschooling, but there is one very difficult thing about it, and that is answering the question "What is a typical day?" The very core of the idea is embracing what comes along. I can tell a couple of stories that might illustrate this method (or lack of method).

One day we were watering the back yard and talking about flow dynamics, although we didn't use that term. We were observing the speed of the flow, and the swirls, and the "materials" (type and condition of soil, angle of the hill, all that stuff). I told my husband he would have *loved* to have grown up in a place where he'd needed to irrigate. Irrigating an orchard or field is a huge thrill for those who like to play in the water.

A few days later the kids and I were on the way to the unschoolers' meeting place, and Kirby (11) had a small water pistol with him. "Is that empty?" I asked.

"No."

"Well please empty it, because some of the other moms won't want their kids to get wet, and it's not a good idea to have water fights where we don't have towels or other clothes."

Ooh, I heard that mom voice and looked at the squirt gun, and it was a five ounce insignificant little thing, but still... So Kirby said he would empty it out the window, which he proceeded to do, squirting it on his hand and discussing how much colder it was to have a wet hand in the wind than dry.

We got to the park to find that five ounces of clean water would have been a drop in a lake, and there the lake was—right under all four swings. The park had been over watered.

As each family showed up I'd ask if they had a shovel. Nope. After half an hour I decided to go and get one. I got two, from two nearby friends' houses, and came back and started to shovel sand into the water. By then, though, kids were swinging and many were already wet from the knees down and happy.

I announced that I was going to move the puddle over, and started digging a trough. Other moms and kids said, "What!?" and came to see, and to help. Hydro-engineering time! Kids and moms took turns with shovels and plastic buckets. We drained and filled the puddles, diverting most of the water into a hole designed for that purpose. It was BIG sandbox play, with fifteen or more participants from babies to middle-aged kids, and as many observers. Sometimes the kids on the swings were dragging their feet in the water to make waves to send down the channel into the new "puddle" so that the swing became a tool in the project as well. Except about gravity, waves and the properties of dry sand vs.

19

wet, there wasn't any "technical" discussion at all, only joking and "This is fun!"

Did that puddle "need" to be moved? It didn't even "need" to be filled in. It was play, a game. I felt the need to try to move a puddle. I would have done it by myself, but it was a blast to have help.

Was it educational? I think it will affect some of those lives forever. Besides the engineering aspect, there was the newness, and the camaraderie of working on a spontaneous project without formal organization, in which people could stop at any moment, change plans and methods without approval, and experiment. The cost of materials was nothing. It was one of those moments (half hours) which is so engrossing that time and place aren't as large and important as they sometimes seem. It was large-scale stress-free cooperation.

This sort of learning experience can't be planned. Had it been written up in advance and put on a schedule it wouldn't have been alive and special.

People ask whether unschooling isn't like unit studies. Perhaps in the same way there are hexagonal and pentagonal patterns in nature it is. Mathematicians didn't design the patterns in flowers and starfish, but they see them and name them after the fact. I see, in retrospect, a "water unit," but the best thing I can see in the future is to remain busy, curious, and open to whatever comes along. Flexibility to pursue tangents and cow trails, and continuing to see the wonder in everyday things will lead to learning experiences without prior planning. A butterfly in the yard is more wonderful than a dusty butterfly pinned in a box, but you can control the one in the box better, as long as you don't want it to fly. At least it will be there when you want to look at it. The one in the yard is on his own schedule.

I'm not recommending that anyone go out and move a puddle. If you tried, you would probably pass right by five better adventures looking for an over-watered park that you might never find. I wish everyone reading this the clarity to recognize opportunities and I hope you have fun stumbling onto those special projects and situations which will be uniquely yours—yours and your children's.

Enchanted Families (June/July 1998)
F.U.N. News (1999)
2002 S.O.S. Conference booklet (2002)
Growing Together online newsletter (2004)

Morning

At your house it will be morning again within 24 hours, but it could be morning in your heart any second.

Somewhere in the world it is morning every moment. Somewhere, light is dawning. Some people, and I'm one of them, believe that any portal to the universe leads to the whole universe, and if that's true we should be able to get to everything in the whole wide world (and beyond) without much effort from something as small as, say, the definition of a word. How about "morning" and its particulars—daybreak, dawn and sunrise?

Every day the sun comes up (unless you're in the Arctic or Antarctic, in which cases your sun-mileage may vary). Every day is a new opportunity. People say that all the time: "It's the dawning of a new day." If you just let those thoughts and truths go by, you're missing something important that happens 365 days a year (sometimes with a bonus round). Don't miss important things like opportunities for renewal and change. At your house it will be morning again within 24 hours, but it could be morning in your heart any second.

"The morning of the world," someone might say, meaning just as the world was new and bright. From this, we and our children can talk about and learn about poetry and figurative speech. "The morning of his life..." when likening a lifetime to a day, with its own first light, eventual afternoon, and twilight. These are common references. "In Queen Victoria's day..."

At our wedding my friends and relatives all sang "Morning Has Broken," and it was the morning of our lives together. Later that day we had three children. Well, later meaning over the next six and a half years. Sometimes time passes slowly, and sometimes it speeds by, and there is a lesson in focus, and in flow, and in biochemistry.

Some people collect bugs, or rocks, or videotapes. It's cheaper and easier to collect words. If you have a name that's a noun, like "Lynn" or "Holly" or "Gill" you've probably developed an ear for hearing it and an eye for seeing it in various contexts and have probably looked it up in dictionaries and name books to see how old it is. This can be done with morning and joy and tree and wind. I should have put quotation marks on those, "morning" and "joy" and so forth, to show that I mean the word morning, not the thing-in-the-sky morning. Now we're talking about punctuation, the mechanics of writing, and the branch of philosophy called ontology, about what "being" is — is the word "morning" part of morning itself? Is morning inside my head? Where does a "real" morning end and just talking and thinking about morning start? Can you pretend morning?

You can spend $20 on a Mensa-approved plastic puzzle, or a book of mind-bending questions, or you can just look out the window, name things, and think.

You can play with a dictionary, ask each other odd questions, and look up the answers. It's the thinking that counts, the idea-getting, the biochemical ping when the light of a new concept dawns in your mind.

When people begin homeschooling, that's a big bright morning, but you can have as many mornings as you need. If you want to change the way you're being or thinking, just do it. Don't wait for another year, another month, another day. Good morning!

Home Education Magazine, July/August 1998
LUNO newsletter (Oregon), August 1998

Bored No More

Another homeschooling mom once wrote, "It's a valuable lesson to learn to deal with boredom, just like all other emotions."

Until I read that, I hadn't ever thought of boredom as an emotion. I liked the idea. When a child comes to me seeking advice on how to deal with any emotional state, I'm flattered and glad for the opportunity.

Traditionally in this culture boredom is seen as a state of sin. "I'm bored" is met by unthinking parents with, "Then mop the kitchen," or "You have a thousand dollars' worth of toys, you can't be bored," or "Boredom's good for you." I believe the VERY common habit of belittling children who use the word "bored" should be rethought (or "thought," since it seems many parents have never considered it carefully but just repeat what their parents said to them).

If a child came and said she was heartbroken would you tell her she was a brat and should clean the garage? If a child came and said he was angry enough to hit would you say, "Then sit down and read a book whether you want to or not"? Wouldn't you try to help them? It's nonsensical to me that some parents shame their children for saying they are at a loss about what to do next.

The most to be accomplished from punishing or sending bored kids away is that the kids will learn not to go to that parent for advice and ideas.

Sometimes the real message behind "I'm bored" is "I'm little and feeling agitated and vaguely unhappy and I don't know what I can do to get over this uncomfortable feeling. What would you do if you were my age, in this house, on a day like this?"

I think that deserves a helpful, respectful response.

It is rare that my children say "I'm bored," but when they do I walk with them where they are, or to some other part of the house, thinking quickly about what I might have that they have never seen, or haven't seen for a while. I think of art supplies or games or toys or musical instruments they haven't thought of for a long time. I scan my mind and the house for things to provide some visual, auditory,

olfactory, or mental stimulation, preferably two or three of those. Tactile stimulation is good too—perhaps the offer of a shower or bath with new/different toys, or different soap or something. Sometimes "watering the yard" (playing with the hose) will do. When a baby cries for no clear reason, parents will often joyfully see whether the baby means "I'm uncomfortable." They'll try a change of clothes, physical contact, a change of temperature, more air, less air, hot food, cold food, a stroll outside, a car ride, *something* different. Older kids have the same needs, and the expression of that need might come through as whining, irritability, or a claim of boredom.

Maybe it's not physical need, but intellectual need. Boredom is a desire for input that unschooling parents should welcome. It's a child saying "How can I add excitement to my life?" This can be a big opportunity to introduce a new subject, activity, or thought-collection.

Maybe it's an emotional need, and the parent's undivided attention for a little while will solve the problem. A walk, some joking, a hug, inquiries about progress on the child's projects or plans or friends might serve many purposes at once. If after a walk and a talk the child is not quite refreshed, you still had that time together, which made "I'm bored" a useful invitation to bonding.

Sometimes "bored" means tired, low on energy, needing a break from conscious thought and responsibility. Arranging a nap, or putting on a soothing video (even for older kids—a romance instead of an action flick, or light drama instead of comedy), leaving a pillow on the couch and herding the rest of the family in other directions might result in an unplanned but needed nap.

I'm grown. I still get bored occasionally. Thinking about why I'm bored and forgiving myself for being bored have helped me assist my children in learning some coping skills they can use in their own lives. I have also used my occasional boredom as a trigger to seek out the kids. If there's a lull in my life now I should fill it with those children who will be gone too soon.

Welcome opportunities to learn about when and why your child asks for your advice and stimulation. The threshold of needing the parent will change over time, and parents can really use knowing where it is and seeing the benefit in it. One complaint of parents of school kids is that communications are lacking or are misunderstood. Homeschoolers have the fulltime luxury of the chance to do better. Unschoolers have the added advantage of "counting" every interaction as a learning experience. Self awareness, interpersonal skills, creativity and compass-sion all come into play when a child and a parent can build an uplifting memory from "I'm bored."

Home Education Magazine in September 1998
Home Education News in British Columbia, January/February 2003
Acorns Volume 7, Issue 7, March 2004

Textbooks for Unschoolers
or "Triviality"

"So you don't use books?"
Like fingernails on a chalkboard (something my children might never experience) that question breaks into a calm day from time to time. By "books" many people mean school-style "text books" designed for one subject area, one "school year," one level. They mean school books.

Even when I know they mean school books I say, "Yes, we use *lots* of books." By then, my nervous system has relaxed from the unexpected screech of the realization that some people think that unchoolers somehow have houses devoid of books.

School-trained adults (like me) have developed an internal school year, and in the fall we might pine for school supplies and new books. I have a suggestion for new unschoolers who feel the book-buying imperative coming upon them, or for experienced unschoolers who have been given money for "supplies" or whose relatives want ideas about what to buy. The good news is there are hundreds of these books. The better news is you can find them used, almost anywhere.

I'm talking about collections of trivia. These are gold and diamond mines for unschooling. I'll name some books we've played with to good advantage, but there are many out there at used book stores and garage sales, or on the shelves of your friends and relatives, and probably some right under your nose.

I have a few personal favorites the kids haven't yet discovered: *The Voice of the Middle Ages in Letters, Royal Anecdotes* and *Eyewitness to History*. Some people might be "tsking" at this moment that those are not trivia books, but they ARE! They are snippets of the best parts of some obscure situations about which a whole book or chapter might never be written. They're books about real things and people and places, but they don't have to be read from beginning to end. In fact, there's no reason to read the whole book. It makes more sense to flip through, open randomly, play with the index. Mine are all filled with sticky notes, marginal marks, and folded corners.

Then there are things to read to children at odd moments, when they're eating, when we're sitting in waiting rooms, driving in the van, or reading someone to sleep. *How to Do Just About Anything*, published by Reader's Digest, was a guessing game on a van trip. I'd start reading the instructions for making or doing, and the kids and my husband would shout out guesses, getting progressively closer until they knew, and I'd start another one. Sometimes they want me to finish what I was reading even though they've guessed. Shish kebabs, short circuits and shower curtains are all on one page! Now that's educational.

Brewer's Dictionary of Phrase & Fable has snippets from songs, stories, riddles, mythology, and literary references which came into public use with a vengeance. Their entry for Nine Man's Morris has the game board illustrated, with instructions for play. The "Whitsun Morris Dance" mentioned in Henry V can be illuminated for your whole family with this book, as can a few thousand other common linguistic details of everyday life.

So what IS trivia, then? For school kids, trivia is (by definition) a waste of time. It's something that will not be on the test. It's "extra" stuff. For unschoolers, though, in the wide new world in which *everything* counts, there can be no trivia in that sense. If news of the existence of sachets ties in with what one learned of medieval plagues in *Extraordinary Endings of Practically Everything and Everybody*, there are two pointers that tie microbiology to European cities in the Middle Ages, and lead to paradise-guaranteed pilgrimages to Rome. Nowadays sanitation and antibiotics keep the plague from "spreading like the plague." [Note: *Extraordinary Endings... and Extraordinary Beginnings...* might not be suitable for young children who read well. Read-aloud can avoid some topics that might not be ideal for pre-teens.]

Looking around my office for another book to name, I see *Fowler's Modern English Usage*. Trivia!? Well if there isn't going to be a test, the history of the word "paraphernalia" is as interesting as the death of Billy the Kid. There are minotaurs and griffons in there too, just for flipping through!

The edition of *The New York Public Library Desk Reference* we have might be a little outdated, but the rules of ice hockey haven't changed, nor the way in which one addresses a letter to the Pope, nor the date of the discovery of Krypton. (Some of you thought it was just a Superman thing, didn't you? Nope—1898, the year before aspirin.)

We have a quiz book on New Mexico. You might find one for your state too. We challenge our adult friends in front of the kids and the kids can't wait to know enough to play. I won us dessert at a restaurant once knowing how many counties there were and the kids were in awe.

Stephen Biesty's cross-sections books, David MacCaulay's *The Way Things Work*, any "What to Do With the Kids..." kinds of books, question/answer books like *The Star Wars Question and Answer Book about Space*, all will fill your kids with more questions than they had before they opened the books. This is good. This is not school-good, but it's unschooling-good. The parents don't have to know the answers, they just need to be willing to help be on the lookout for a source to come along within the next few months or years.

Doing the Days might be a good intro book for those afraid to embark upon the sea of trivia. (Have you looked up the history of the word "embark"? Any word history book will enthrall your whole family.) It's a set of activities divided out by days of the year, designed to encourage thinking and doing in children. I never pay attention to the dates much, just mine it for trivia!

2201 Fascinating Facts is well worth the dollar I paid for it, and *The Book of Fascinating Facts* by Encyclopedia Britannica is worth the whole $13 I paid for it on sale at Toys 'R Us because it has over 350 pages of COLOR PICTURES. Life-size photo of a human stomach, a 1930's typewriter with the paper half typed and legible in it, and singing cowboys. Every one of those leads us to pull out another book, or a record, or to go dig in the garage.

Visual dictionaries, books of birds, mammals, local flora, the dictionary, encyclopedia, atlas, almanac—these books can be used by the hour or by the half minute. There is no time wasted when children are thinking, asking questions, fitting new information with what they already have, and all the while smiling and laughing. Have fun!

Home Education Magazine, November/December 1998.
Gastfreundschaft, Western Australia, Winter 2003

Lego knights on the patio

How Elvis Appears to Unschoolers

Once long ago, in 1993, on Prodigy's Homeschooling bulletin board, I wrote this, and it conjured Elvis:

> Some time back there was a request for songs to be sung which would be educational. As music itself is a discipline, I think any music can be used as an educational tool. It can tie in with physical activity, mathematics, physics, history, geography, art, language, and it can be used to get kids excited and awake, or calm and asleep, or anything in between. I don't mean singing about math or history, either, but discussing the form of the music, the rhythm, the moods, the origins, the instruments on which it is traditionally played, the length and pattern of the verses (or phrases, or whatever), what its purpose is (a march, background music for a movie or for an 18th century fireworks show, a lullaby, a love song), etc.
>
> Don't miss this fun and easy opportunity to tie different "subjects" together by using a song as a jumping off place to many different discussions. If you need ideas, name a song here and see how many suggestions you can get for it!

So that sat out in public for nearly two hours before someone wrote, "Ok, I'll try that. 'Blue Suede Shoes'."

I had never been an Elvis fan. Still, it was rich with potential. The next ten paragraphs here were the response:

> Look up pictures of the 50's. What was happening in those days? Where did Elvis Presley come from?
>
> What was the deal with Black music in those days? What was new that benefited Elvis's career? (Television! Cheap color movies!)
>
> How was his induction into the army (combined with his popularity) used by the government? Find some old magazines with articles showing him in uniform, in his barracks, etc.
>
> What is suede, anyway? How is it made? How far back in history was there suede? How is leather tanned? How would suede be made blue? How does dye work? (Visit Tandy leather, or a shoe repair place. Tie-dye something.)

Talk about slang. Much of what was slang in the 50's is mainstream English now. What is slang that hasn't yet died out or been accepted by a larger group?

"One for the money, two for the show, three to get ready and [go, cat] go": With "four to go," what is that used for outside this song? Is it fair to just steal words from just anywhere for song lyrics? Sure it is! Look for some other examples. (It might take months of casual listening to find another example, but there are lots.)

What is "slander"? (Check "libel".)

If the children are trained in music, you can talk about syncopation. If they're up on music technology, discuss the simple mixing that went on at recording studios in the 50's and early 60's, before stereo was common (and before mono was no more). Listen to the quality of the bass line and compare it to a modern recording with a broader spectrum and newer technology on storage and playback. Find something that explains how magnetic tape works for sound recording and CD's and phonograph records. (Usborne's music and science books have some stuff about this, and encyclopedias have too.)

What instrument did Elvis Presley play? Do you have a guitar at your house, and could the kids learn a few chords? (Blue Suede Shoes can be played with four, I think, in a simplified form.) What other instruments are on the recording? What time signature is the song in? What key? How could you find out? (pitch pipe, keyboard)

What's the difference between rock'n'roll and jazz? Blues? (This might be easier by identifying samples-—i.e. multiple choice—than by definition.)

These are just the things I'm thinking of as fast as I can type. Some would be too hard for some kids, some might not interest the parents or kids, but every one could lead to something else, which could lead to something else again. Looking through old *Life* or *Look* magazines would reveal lots of civil rights activity, the Korean War, the first days of Camp David, advertisements for modern gas appliances, discussions of the new suburban homes (40-yr-old houses, shown as brand new cutting-edge technology), and advertisements for automobiles (with the prices, even in those days), and Elvis might be just a tiny thought on the side of learning about the 50's. How did I do? Others should add more!

So, back to the present now, I was amazed at how much had poured out. That led to my "Everything is Educational" belief which has turned into folders and workshops. Elvis had finally really captured my attention.

A few years later my kids asked about Hawaii and were amazed that I was already alive when Hawaii became a state and remembered reading about it in Weekly Reader at school. "Tell us more." I thought of Elvis again, and went and rented *Blue Hawaii.* We ate pineapple. I found an umbrella I had bought at a thrift shop that was manufactured in Hawaii before statehood. That started our "unit" on Hawaii, but as I explained things to them ideas were coming together and being taken apart in my own mind.

When *Blue Hawaii* was new, Americans were seeing some of their first BIG, color photos of Hawaii, and some of their first moving footage. TV was still in black and white, and newspapers were too. Even most magazines were full of black and white photographs.

We talked about Germany, the Berlin Wall, prejudice, colonization, plantations, volcanoes, latitude, oceanography, music, fashion, realities in wealthy families that don't apply to poorer families, cultural traditions, the changing culture after WWII... We talked about commercial airlines, engineering and economics. We got more out of a movie that was never intended (except for the tolerance and anti-prejudice messages) than I expected we would. And still I left things out. The actress wasn't really half Hawaiian (I'm guessing), but I left that for my kids to figure out later on their own.

Part of what this sort of exploration takes is the willingness to let go of an "outline" or of a hope that you will find something, and an ability to go with what you do find. It's the big airplane hangar door to unschooling, through which, if you can leave the schoolish building your own mind has built, that has "academics" sorted and stacked against old walls with bad memories, you can see that light of the real world outside. Just move out toward those cliffs and flowers and see what kind of birds are out there.

So take up a glass of pineapple juice while "Blue Suede Shoes" blares in the background. Here's hoping you see Elvis soon!

Home Education Magazine, January/February 1999

The back corner of our house, viewed over the hood
of Keith's old turquoise Dodge truck.

Leaning on a Truck
and other parallel play

Women talk face to face, they say, but men lean side by side on a truck. Another version of leaning on a truck is fishing: facing the same way, doing the same thing. Traditionally these days parents and children move in different spheres and do different things, but unschooling families mix ages and activities.

What can be the model of parent/child interaction? Well there's the time-honored "riding in the car," a *great* time and place for humor, news, and deep conversation. With a tape player, you get music, stories, and grand lyrics about the history of the world and faraway places. But people can't live in the car. Washing dishes is a great time to sing or tell stories, but even after the biggest holiday dinner, the dishwashing ends. Raking leaves is a great project to lend itself to talking while doing.

Inside the house, though, I have discovered the motherlode of two-for-ones, of tools for inspiring and sustaining conversation. I suppose you have some of these things, or might want to put them on your wish list. My favorite is pattern blocks. There are some hardwood blocks stained in a few bright colors, available for $25 at educational supply stores and upscale toyshops. They are mesmerizing. We bought a second set after a while so we could fill the table with one big mandala pattern after another. And over those blocks my children have told their secret dreams, and we have discussed art and math, manufacturing, stain and paint, we have laughed and been silent. While the blocks were still out our children have dazzled visiting adults with their dexterity and artistic sense, then they've wandered off and the visitors have talked to me, while making patterns with blocks, about things that might have been hard to discuss if we were sitting facing one another. They've discussed their fears and love lives and embarrassments, and made some really great patterns.

Jigsaw puzzles are wonderful, and you can get them at yard sales and thrift stores for less than a dollar. Greeting cards cost $2 now, but you can get a thousand-piece jigsaw puzzle for 50¢, so what does it matter if it might have a piece or three missing? Cheaper than a greeting card. Work it and throw it away. While you're working it, the picture on the box will inspire questions, stories, ideas, tangents. The shapes of the pieces will remind people of other connections in their lives. Except for those toddlers who eat puzzle pieces, puzzles can  involve people of all ages together. There are some on the market now with big pieces at one end, medium in the middle, and small for the rest. Some bright parent thought THAT up. They'll be coming soon to a yard sale near you.

 At a thrift store I got some castle building blocks made in Spain, about which many a grown man has said, "I wish I had these when I was a boy!" They're especially interesting to adults who've seen castles, read about them, and who can set the portcullis up without looking at the instructions. And while they're building castles, they're talking about fishing or trucks or computers or the dangers of amateur fire-eating.

Over the years we have collected magnets in one plastic cup—leftovers from various games, magnet sets, things found in parking lots, etc. Sometimes the magnets come out, and nobody passes without playing. Nobody plays without sitting and talking.

For Christmas I got a miniature Zen garden. Leaving it out for all comers has been enlightening for definite sure. Some people do very western-style patterns.

Some have obviously seen Zen gardens or at least photos, because they'll pull the rocks out and make a pile of sand for a focal point. "It's just like an Etch-a-Sketch," I heard once. We've discussed the difference in the sand at various beaches, how it's "mined" by the Rio Grande, and what that stuff really is at White Sands down by Alamogordo, where the grandparents live.

We have made good use of making patterns in the slots of a revolving rack of poker chips, and then with poker chips out on the table. I have set out photo-copied pictures and cheap watercolors, lots of brushes, and had side-by-side painting by the hour. Whichever kids or visitors wander by will be drawn in and as they play or paint they talk and share and think.

Some families are less likely to play than others. Some adults have forgotten how. I treasure the moments when a recently-schooled older child has snorted at the "daily special" out on the table, but on seeing an adult pick up the modeling wax or the tops which are really felt tip pens and leave a pink squiggly trail, or whatever cool thing is out, they sit, play and talk.

So this talkin'—what is it good for? Everything in the whole wide world. If I planned to talk specifically about castles during castle block days, I might have missed the discussion of why one little girl is jealous of other friends and how she might best be encouraged to play in groups. We might not have discussed compost piles while playing with magnets had I said that what animals eat has nothing to do with magnetism.

Toothpicks and miniature marshmallows—now *there* is a bonding activity. I recommend against using such words as "angles" and "pyramids" though, and just let conversation flow to sugar, campfires, trees, squirrels, Volkswagens, Utah, sandstone, soapstone, tobacco, sailing ships and the Spanish Armada. If you call it "geometry" you might not get all the way to England with it.

So why does this work? Let us assume (with my house as an example, at least) that hyperactivity runs in families and that like attracts like. With extra energy, people can do two things at once. If one of those things is pattern-building and physical, that whole verbal part of the brain is still available. Working on patterns in silence allows one's mind to whirl and twirl. Doing something non-verbal while talking has a special advantage: Silence is not awkward. Changing the subject temporarily to talk about the blocks or paints or puzzle is not really changing the subject. Fear and foreboding won't cause people to leave the conversation or cry. It's possible to pause, think, breathe, stall, collect oneself and come back to the topic in a minute. I have a near-teen here who sometimes needs to be with me a while before he gets to what he needs to say. That puzzle didn't really need to be worked, but perhaps that child needed to sit with that parent.

I can't predict what will be discussed the next time you set out some engrossing bowl of shells or foreign coins, or a box of buttons, or the antique Tinker Toys you got at the garage sale, but if you sit there long enough, the talking will start and I don't think you'll be disappointed.

Home Education Magazine, March-April 1999
My children were 12, 10 and 7.

Your House as a Museum

Once my kids were watching something or other on TV about woodcuts and block printing, and somehow the subject turned to printed cloth. I told them I had some block-printed cloth and they got pretty excited about seeing it.

I found an Indian bedspread, printed in two passes, with blocks, and we looked at where they had made some great matches, where they had missed, and how it all might work (because I don't know what their work stations look like, whether they do edges first, or what). I found two scarves made of fine cotton, block-printed each in one color only. Then I found some screen-printed silk handkerchiefs from China that a friend had given me after his mother died. Still in the packages, and some matching pairs, so we could compare. They might have been mass produced, but still... Then I found a piece of Hawaiian cloth. I don't know the name of it, but my husband's mom brought it from Hawaii. I think it's a kind of Polynesian kilt.

I also had a piece of woven paisley, a batik sari and a sari with gold woven into it. I didn't go into detail about those except to point out that most of those examples were made in India. Someday I'll read them *The Road to Agra* which is a kids' adventure novel and which deals in passing with the child labor involved in weaving.

With that my children decided that anything they might want to see, I would have. There have been many times that they were right!

When they asked what pogs were supposed to be *really*, I found an old milk-bottle that had been stuck up in the top of a cabinet just in case a kid might ever want to see it, next to the old molded Pepsi bottle, and the not-so-old Coca Cola bottle. I told them stories of picking up bottles to turn in for the two-cent deposit. It's the equivalent of picking up aluminum cans now, but they're heavy and fragile. The kids had never known about bottle deposits like that, where the bottles were reused instead of melted down. I told them about people throwing bottles out of car windows on the highways, and all the broken glass we walked on and around as kids, and that people used to shoot at bottles for practice.

Kids nowadays take "Keep American Beautiful" for granted. They can't believe there used to be rusting bedsprings and old washing machines dumped all over the place, and that hamburger wrappers were as likely as not to go out the window of a car. I told them about how the old glass would weather, and what had been in the sand and sun of New Mexico for long enough would turn into smooth-edged, opaque little jewels we used for hopscotch markers. Pogs to hopscotch—full circle, because I had those bottles.

My maiden name was Adams, and I remember being taunted by kids singing the theme song to *The Addams Family* TV show, but that line "Their house is a museum where people come to see 'em" stuck with me always. When I go to other people's houses I love to see what they have. The things they've chosen to keep, or collected over the years, teach me a good deal about those people themselves—their interests, their history, their sense of humor, and philosophy.

Sometimes my kids get bored, and I can light up a half hour by digging into some box or drawer and producing something they've never yet seen. Like a magician pulling a bouquet of flowers out of a wand, I pull out a little doll, or some Australian coins, electric curlers (for sorting, putting back on the rods, and discussing), muffin tins, poker chips, grandpa's bow ties, a hand-cranked egg beater to froth up soapy water (I wish I had a hand-cranked drill; my dad did). Whenever I pull these things out I tell the kids why I have them and what I know about them. I told about the gold strip in Australian paper money, about ties my dad used to have with cowboys and bucking broncos on them, about patterned muffin tins being pressed kind of like steel car parts are pressed, of getting my hair stuck in electric curlers when I was a teenager and crying because I was afraid my long hair would have to be cut off.

Can you remember visiting grandparents or older relatives when you were young and finding cool "stuff" in their store-rooms? My granny had "carding combs" I think she called them—steel brushes for cleaning cotton and lining up the fibers. She'd never spun, as far as I know, but she would use raw cotton to put into quilts, taking the seeds out herself and carding the cotton. When my mom was little, their whole family had picked cotton by hand for a living, moving from town to town in West Texas. My other grandmother, my Mamaw, had an ironing machine, and said they used to iron sheets and pillow cases with it.

There are probably things in your house that would fascinate your children but you haven't thought to offer or they haven't found the good stuff yet. Consider interesting things you have that might be of interest for being old, foreign, specially made or obtained under special circumstances:

ornaments
dishes / pots /molds
silverware—even one old piece you know something about
egg beater
flour sifter
can openers ("church keys")
old bottles or other containers
old clothes from the 60's or 70's
recordings—reel to reel, 45's, 78's, 8-tracks
manual typewriter
push mower
pre-transistor radio
musical instruments
jewelry (and any old photos of people wearing that actual jewelry)
photos of people with cars (I try to get cars in photos to date them)
books, magazines
clippings
ribbons from 4-H, scout badges, school certificates, class photos, report cards
toys from your childhood
awards / trophies (photos of the activity?)
funeral cards
wedding announcements/certificates
birth announcements
games (any old Monopoly games in your attic?)
teach clapping games or jump rope (living-history museum stuff!)
foods no longer commonly used (find a fondue pot and make them something)
poker chips (patterns, counting, sorting)
sewing supplies / buttons
old shoes
uniforms
curlers / bobby pins
drafting supplies
typewriter eraser with a brush
old pens, paper, ancient stationery
flip-open address book like people had on desks in 1963
old phone
old phonebook or school annual with alpha prefixes—
    find out what your local prefix used to be (if it's old enough)
art
music
things relating to WWII, Korea, Viet Nam

Many people in the southwest have wagon wheels. They're not flat—the hub is out at an angle from the wheel, and the spokes hold it at that angle for strength and stability. It's fascinating to look at one, and touch it, and know that it took an experienced wheelwright to make that wheel, and a blacksmith to put the iron on it, and that the very wheel came here from somewhere else—maybe Mexico, maybe Missouri, maybe Kansas. It was made somewhere, and came here, and now it's sitting in someone's yard.

Do you have rocks or mineral samples?
Do you have an emerald or a ruby or a diamond?
Do you have a really old camera?
Any leather-bound books or boxes?

My husband has something the kids haven't seen yet—a set of bongo drums.

So what's at your house?

Home Education Magazine, May/June 1999

Learning Against My Will
(or "Input, Please!")

I've missed two columns, and it's not because Dee Sanchez isn't the sweetest most patient editor in the world. I was having unscheduled learning opportunities. These educational experiences are all over the place lately. I'd kinda like to sleep.

My children don't go to school. The boys are 12 and 10, and lately they have been obsessed with a game they borrowed, *Warcraft II*, which they play on a Macintosh right next to mine. This has been great for me, because just as with the "parallel play" of toddlers, we're together, but have nothing to fight about. Well hardly anything. They want me off the phone sometimes so they can call their friends and brag about how many pixellated orcs they killed. And I would like to listen to Prince, or Donovan, and they whine "I can't hear the game, mom…"

So if I'm sitting right there at a computer why am I not writing the most important thing in my life, a column for *Enchanted Families*? Because there are people interested in learning, and they're asking me questions.

One of the finest ways to clarify a concept is to explain it to someone else. It's one thing to passively understand (at least momentarily in short-term memory) how to tie a clove hitch or to make waffles, but to really know the thing you need to have done it so much you can do it while you're sleepy, in the dark, in a wind storm. Or so much that you could pass the secret skill on to another person. Be prepared for the most important question of all: "Why?"

Sometimes the people asking "why" are my children. Sometimes they're friends who come over, or call. Often they're people (friends, acquaintances, strangers) who e-mail me for information. At the moment I have outstanding questions in my e-mail inbox about sources for polyphonic Christmas music for beginners; a detail from pre-1978 about awards given in an organization I joined in those days; an inquiry as to whether a friend fell off the planet (no, he just got laid off and so hasn't been checking e-mail); whether hermits can practice virtue or whether it takes other humans to practice on; what were Anglo-Saxon women's names like? By "outstanding" I don't just mean *great* questions, but questions I haven't yet had time or inspiration to answer fully. While I'm willing to say "I don't know" when it's true, these are things about which I do have some knowledge. All I have to do is write in some detail what the people want to know.

At least my kids don't require me to write out the answers to their questions. We keep a running commentary on one another's lives, and so what I'm learning trickles down to them, and their questions make me think like crazy.

Crazy-thinking isn't bad.

I'm writing this two days before leaving to speak at a conference in southern California. My session is called "Permission to Think Without Permission." It might seem silly, but most people seem to feel unauthorized to think wildly. Mixing and matching thoughts will stir up things you had forgotten you had remembered. Like emptying out a closet full of cool stuff and sorting through it to show your kids things you had forgotten you had, just messing with ideas and answering unusual questions will be a learning experience for all concerned, and will produce more and different brain trails.

And that sleep I wanted? In the three days I worked on and off on this little missive, I slept a lot, and had the most wonderful dreams. If I had told you about them we could talk for hours, and we'd all be thinking new and interesting thoughts.

I'd like to recommend a book you might have to special order, but you won't regret it if you do: *The Book of Learning and Forgetting* by Frank Smith, Teachers College Press, Columbia University, 1998. ISBN: 0-8077-3750-X. It's about how people learn—how easily and effortlessly natural learning is, and how difficult-to-impossible "formal education" is compared to the real learning that goes on every day of a person's life. If your family's priority is learning, you can spend time in no better way than playing with and rearranging the ideas you already have and incorporating bits of what you see, hear, smell, taste, feel and think.

Enchanted Families, May/June 1999
(and yes, it did end kind of abruptly)

Zoombini Excitement

Unschoolers' Coming-Out Parties
Wishlists for Unschoolers

I usually write non-fiction, but this time I'm deep into fantasy.

What if new homeschoolers were welcomed to their new lives with elaborate parties and mounds of thoughtfully chosen gifts? Take a moment before you read on to think what you would like to have had in your pile of loot.

Ah...

And then think about the special particulars of ideal gifts for unschoolers!

This idea came to me from a La Leche League meeting at which our wise and experienced leaders ran a similar scenario: "If you could give the perfect gift to a new nursing mother, what might it be?" The favored answer was "a rocking chair."

I've asked this question of some other unschoolers on occasion, and they sigh wistfully. Most bought things they never used, when they were new at unschooling, and would like their hundreds of dollars back. Many find the idea that others would be not only supportive but help them materially in this way a near-inconceivable situation that exists in dream-only mode.

Here's my collected wish list:

Local contacts and introductions. People. Hook them up with other families with experienced unschooled kids. A newsletter or state magazine, either some back issues or a subscription, would give them something to read and to show the relatives. A major homeschooling magazine subscription would be great in addition to local contacts. If they already get *Home Education Magazine*, they could use *Growing Without Schooling* (or your back issues, at least).[1]

A catalog and a gift certificate to go with it would combine loot and math! There are probably advertisements right in the magazine you're holding for suppliers of books, games, science and geography treasures, music, stories on tape or art supplies. If you have a favorite catalog, no doubt your new unschooling friend would like it too. Catalogs without gift certificates wouldn't hurt either.

Pattern tiles, magnets, puzzles, kits and other such fiddlin'-around stuff are good for children and adults both. They create opportunities for parents and children to interact in wordless or talkative ways, as suits the moment.

---

[1] At publication, the two unschoolingest magazines are *Live Free Learn Free* and *Life Learning*.

Games can be the finest gifts of all. You might find used games at garage sales or thrift stores (for gift giving or your own family). Mastermind for Kids is cute. Yahtzee is cheap and good. Ravensburger makes some very attractive games. Several kids-book publishers have put out excellent chess books for beginners. If you can find a book on the history of games that would help build an interest and historical and geographical connections.

I'd love to give videos of movies that are easy to mine for places, time, and thoughts: *The King and I* with Yul Brynner; *The Ten Commandments* with Yul Brynner (okay, with Charlton Heston); *El Cid* with Charlton Heston; *Ben Hur*! (One thing leads to another in idea getting and fantasy gift-giving.)

Some people could give lists of their greatest ideas, or a list of greatest lists. "Take binoculars with you on trips." "Freeze water in milk cartons to make ice sculptures later." "Rearrange your books sometimes just to stir them up."

Sing-along videos for families with small children serve several purposes. The songs and art are usually high quality, and the words are scrolling by. Don't mention anything to the children about reading lessons, but there they'll be, words associated with their sound, in an entirely stress-free environment.

Good, real art supplies and maybe some idea-books or friendly personal introduction to their use would be a luxury some kids have never had. Good watercolors and real brushes and special paper, instead of grocery-store stuff might make the difference in a child's future.

Lens-stuff: a good magnifying glass, a telescope, microscope, or binoculars and an article or book on how lenses work, and what might be seen or done with optical tools.

I could comment on everything below at length, but you can probably construct your own explanations and ideas on such categories as:

  * good toys
  * computer games
  * recorded music
  * interesting storage containers
  * exotic foodstuffs
  * bookshelves
  * songbooks
  * dress-up clothes and hats
  * logic puzzles (verbal or physical)
  * crafts books
  * science experiments
  * real scissors
  * a binder full of sheet protectors for kid-art
  * magazine subscriptions for kid-hobbies or interests

* disposable camera and film developing
* books for identifying local flora and fauna
* passes to museums
* maps
* highlighters
* seashells for desert kids
* interesting rocks for city kids
* a musical instrument or two
* a current globe and a really old one

Looking back on the list of suggestions, I realize it's still not fantastic (fantasy-like) enough for me. Those things are available all over the place.

What if you could give magical gifts? How about the ability to change bodies long enough to see the world as your children see it? Perhaps just a few doses of magic to make time stand still, for just a little while. More time and space? Unlimited patience! Friendly neighbors. A perpetually well-running van in the mom's favorite color. Intuitive knowledge of child development would be a good gift for homeschoolers and all their friends, neighbors and relatives. If you figure out how to produce such gifts, please remember me after your friends have all they need.

For my wish list, throw in that big, soft rocking chair too.

Home Education Magazine, July/August 1999

Kirby and Holly

Bringing Shakespeare Home

Song lyrics are meant to be sung, recipes are made to be cooked, and Shakespeare is made to be performed and watched. Reading Shakespeare from a book is an American school tradition, but it makes less sense than reading recipes you never intend to cook or taste.

Shakespeare is the fodder for many graduate degrees, and can be one's life's work, but it's not the big mystery some would like you to think it is. With very little expense or effort you can introduce your family to Shakespeare and if they have a sparkly interest, with another few dozen dollars or so (less than the cost of one college course) you can all become experts.

Here is the secret: *rent videos*. That's easy. If you're around big video rental stores, you'll have no problem. If you're out in the country, you might need to use interlibrary loan, or mailorder some videos. The wonderful thing about videos is that you can pause, rewind, turn them off and think for a few days. You can pause and look things up. You can pause and call your friend who knows about Shakespeare.

Shakespeare's plays are categorized as histories, tragedies and comedies. Here's my recommendation for a basic starter set. If you watch these and discuss them with your family, the kids will have had a better introduction to Shakespeare than most high school students have ever had in the U.S. All are readily available for rent. For the tragedy, choose *Romeo and Juliet* (Zeffirelli, 1968) or *Hamlet* (the one with Mel Gibson—Zeffirelli, 1990). History: *Henry V* (Branagh, 1989). Comedy: *Much Ado About Nothing* (Branagh, 1993) or *Twelfth Night* (Nunn, 1997).

Either buy used or check out from the library a Shakespeare collection (or individual little books of plays if you find those cheaper) so you can see what the plays look like on paper—what stage directions they have, who the characters are, and what sorts of things are edited out to keep the play under two hours. If that seems interesting you can rent the Branagh *Hamlet* (1997), which has the entire text and lasts nearly four hours. If the text you've found has introductory material and footnotes that's best. If you have choices, I'd recommend *The Riverside Shakespeare*. If you have a "Complete Works of Shakespeare" of some sort without notes, look (in used bookstores first) for Cliff's Notes or Monarch Notes for the play. Those will discuss characters and summarize the action.

Another source for information is a book that tells the stories in prose form. One is by Charles and Mary Lamb, *Tales of Shakespeare*. You might find others. You don't have to read that to the kids, you could just read it yourself so you can help explain the action if the videos confuse them.

If you have the opportunity to take your children to a live performance, even a student production, that's another good plan, but New Mexico isn't a hotbed of Shakespearean production. *[Author's note: This was first published locally in Albuquerque, on paper, thence the comments above and below.]*

If you have access to the internet, poking around for Shakespearean sites might be fun for you and your children. Try the *Shakespearean Insult Generator* or *Green Eggs and Hamlet*, both of which went around by e-mail in the pre-web-page days of yore.

After you've gone that far, you will probably have come upon lots of books about Shakespeare's life, videos of other plays, related art, music, and humor—all sorts of things. There is an incredible book on Shakespeare for $10 from Usborne books. It would be the best I'd ever seen if it were three times that price. My oldest, when he knew I was writing this, suggested the new *Romeo + Juliet* with Leonardo DiCaprio and Claire Danes. Parental guidance is advised on that one, but my 11-year-old son watched it straight through and understood it and recommends it. I'd start with the period setting (the Zeffirelli) first before going to modern setting, personally.

At that point you could quit forever and your children would have enough exposure to Shakespeare to know whether they would like to pursue it further. If you keep all the activities light and fun, nothing forced or treated as a required bit of drudgery, you might find that you *and* your children will be on the lookout for opportunities to see more Shakespeare and to find trivia and history between plays and movies. Have fun!

Enchanted Families, June (?) 1999
Kootenay Home Educators, Fall 1999

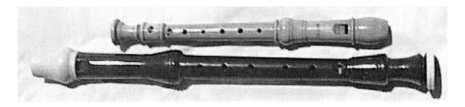

Later notes:
 A good source of information on video or DVD versions is Amazon.com. Look up any Shakespeare play there, and click on one of the lists on the right-hand side. There should be several people's lists of favorite Shakespeare videos with commentary/review, and will be up to date, unlike this book and this even-older article. Also, you can find the texts of the plays online and might not need to get a paper copy at all.

Tiny Monsters

I used to have a four year old. Well, I've had three of them, but on February 2, 1991, four-year-old Kirby came and asked me for a bandaid because his finger had started hurting all by itself. On the second joint there was a little red welt. I asked if he had burned it, and he said no. I asked if maybe an ant or a spider had bitten him, and he said no. I talked a little bit about that, and he said, "If it might be a little tiny monster, I *quit*."

I remember having had that "I *quit*" feeling when I got my first paper cut at the age of five. My Aunt Mona had just given me a big Bible-story book. I was sitting at my granny's kitchen table in Fort Worth, Texas. Thrilled to be the owner of a new book, I opened it expecting glory and wonder and one of the first few pages cut my finger. What a shock to learn that things I'd thought were really safe before that could make me hurt and bleed—I figured then if books were dangerous, the whole world was a much more dangerous place than I was comfortable being in. Here I still am, though, and I was right.

Danger isn't very comfortable. There are roller-coaster moments, and daring-saves moments. There are social-stand-taking moments and belief-defending moments. Those are times we make a conscious (even if hasty) decision to participate. Over and around self-imposed danger there are tiny monsters.

Paper cuts and spider bites are nothing compared to fear and doubt. When someone says, "Are you sure you know what you're doing?" that can hurt for a month or a year. In Disney's *Hercules*, Phil rhymes "disappointment" with "pain for which there ain't no ointment." Sometimes people can disappoint us.

Find encouragement, whether it is from friends, relatives, inspirational books, faith, online bulletin boards, or the smiles of the children in your life. Avoid tiny monsters. Sometimes they will find you, but there's no sense setting your picnic on an ant bed. If someone has repeatedly caused you pain and isn't responding to requests to stop, take a little longer getting back with them next time. Don't stay as long once you get there.

Don't let fear and doubt make you quit. If you're walking up a trail and there's a big rock in the way, do you just turn around and go home? Go around it. Climb over it. Move it. Sit on it and rest. The rock isn't the trail. The rock isn't the destination. It's just a rock. On that hike, it was an unforeseen little monster.

I have something of a monster antidote: breathing. Breathe deeply and calmly. Get oxygen into that part of you that fears the tiny monsters. Once you master calming your hurts and fears (or at least calming the adrenaline that would make you lash out), you'll have time to think about how to deal with them rationally and sweetly and compassionately.

Parents would like to protect their children from all tiny monsters, but it can't be done. One of the greatest gifts you might give your child, your family and yourself is to learn to set an example of how to deal with surprise wounds and doubts, and to coach your children through their encounters with fear and disappointment with calming touch, cleansing breath, and shared hope.

We can't have safety but we can have peace and joy despite the tiny monsters.

Enchanted Families, July/August 1999
Kootenay Home Educators, Winter 1999

Knowing Everything

Holly, who is seven years old, wanted to go to Sunday School. I grew up Baptist, but don't go to church now unless for special music somewhere or other. I took her to Hillside Community Church, an independent Albuquerque church with the motto "Where East meets West." There was a marimba band playing that day, and Sunday School is during the church service, so I was happy.

I rushed to collect Holly from Sunday School so she could see the totally all-wooden marimba, which was resounding with Caribbean recessional music.

On the way out there was a Japanese painting on the wall, with the names of financial contributors around it. I said, "Let's look at the Zen painting." We looked a bit, and on the way to the car Holly said, "What's Zen?"

It's hard enough to discuss "what's Zen" with adults. I stalled and stammered, and she said, "Because there's Zen art, and there are Zen gardens." We have a miniature Zen garden I got for Christmas, and it's out on the counter or kitchen table almost all the time. Once last summer at the unschoolers' play group Holly cleared a place in the sand box, imported some rocks, and made a Zen garden on the playground, explaining to the other kids what she was doing.

Still, I'm balking at trying to explain this to Holly. I said, "It's hard to explain, but I'll try."

"How did your mom explain it to you?"

Upon occasion I think my kids are "behind" because a memory flashes in of me having known something specific at the age one of them is. It's usually something like long division, or the story of Jane Addams or Teddy Roosevelt, or something that seemed vitally important at the time I learned it, and something to be proud of knowing. I remember getting good grades.

Here is a seven year old asking in a very mature way for some information on something I knew NOTHING of until I was in my late teens, and didn't under-stand until I was in my thirties (not that I totally understand it now, but I got over total bafflement eventually). I realized how common this is at our house.

When Kirby was five years old, I read him a picture book about service stations. A while later he came to me and said in a very serious way, "Mom, why are you always telling us everything about this planet?"

"Like what?" I asked, knowing he was asking a real question.

"Like trucks and stuff. Is it because you want us to grow up to be smart mans?"

"Uh huh" (stalling for time to think of a good answer).

"And we can tell *our* kids?"

He already knew the answer. He just wanted some confirmation.

In the week following the Zen day, Holly has asked for definitions of "dignity" (because of a line Lillith delivered to Frazier on late-night TV) and of "sarcastic" (after a friend had said "Sorry, that was sarcastic"). Those were easy to explain compared to Zen. She also asked why "pillow" is called "pillow." She wanted the etymology of the word, so one adult sat and speculated with her while another went and looked it up in a big dictionary. She actually cared about the explanation.

Do you know where I learned a lot of what I know? From my kids. Here is a confession of a large failing, but it turned out well. It is an account of Marty, my middle child, who looked so wise the day he was born. At the age of three he was, in words, teaching me to be a better mother. I have it in my diary, dated Monday, Oct 26, 1992:

> I was putting Kirby and Marty to bed because they were playing really rough and I was grouchy and tired. Marty wouldn't help put things away, wouldn't help set up his bed, and Kirby was doing most of the work. Then Marty was playing a kazoo and I told him to put it away. He put it down on a shelf by his bed and then in just a few seconds he was honking away full force and I said, "Put the kazoo away." He just looked at me and kept playing it. I said, "Marty, I told you to stop. Put it away." He didn't. I said "I'm getting really grouchy about this stuff today. You don't do what I ask you to do." He didn't stop. I swatted him on the thigh and said, "Put it away." He started crying and I swatted him again, and yelled, "You still have the kazoo! Put it away" and I took it out of his hand, but squeezed his fingers in the process, and he was crying. I went to put a cassette tape on and said to both of them "Hitting wasn't a good idea. I'm sorry I hit you, Marty. I couldn't think of the best thing to do. I couldn't think of a good-mom thing to do because I was mad. What do you guys think I should have done?"

> Marty said, "I know what to do, mom, when it's in your arms and in your legs." Marty was, at the age of three, describing an angry rush of adrenaline.

> "What?"

> "Just breathe. Breathe deep breaths." That was the trick I had taught the kids, something I learned when I learned meditation. Oxygen will calm someone down.

> Kirby (who was five and a half) said "I know what. Just ignore it."

"Just ignore that he was playing the kazoo after I told him not to?"

"Yeah."

Marty said with some excitement—"I have the best superdy-duperdy idea and it's in my head"—pointing with both hands to his forehead.

"What is it?"

"You should just play *with* us." (very matter-of-factly said)

"Play with you with the kazoo?"

"Yeah!"

I said, "I'm going to go write these ideas down so the next time I get mad I'll think about them."

In the years since then I have thought about those ideas a lot. Instead of being my mother's child, I am my children's mother.

My mother did the best she could, I suppose. I need to do the best I can do. So I tell my children everything they want to know. I show them the world in words and pictures and music. While they're becoming better, wiser people, I am too. I wish I had learned these things before they were born, but I didn't have my teachers yet. I have tried to pass on to other moms the best of what works well for us, and to put little warning beacons near pitfalls.

My children discuss behavior and social interactions as easily as they discuss Nintendo or their own cats and dogs. When I was their age, psychology, comparative religion and anthropology were far in my future. My kids might not have much formal terminology, but they're extremely conversant and certainly can think in those areas without knowing they're too young (by the book) to do so. They understand well that there are many versions of historical events. They understand that there are different ways to act in different situations, and with people who have particular beliefs and preferences. Some adults could use knowing that.

A few nights ago I had a good example of Zen for Holly. I had already told her that one aspect of Zen is setting up words or visuals designed to surprise a person into thinking something he'd never thought before, but I hadn't had examples I thought she would understand. Here was my example: "It's like a sword that can't cut itself, or..." and as I said "or" and was going to say a mirror that can't reflect itself, her "or" came right on top of mine, and she finished "or Gudrun looking at herself in the mirror?"

I shuddered. I hadn't said "mirror" but I was thinking it. Gudrun is our year-old dog-pound Australian cattle dog. Holly elaborated: "When Gudrun looks in the mirror she doesn't know whether she's seeing another dog or herself."

53

I didn't go into whether a dog has Buddha nature. It wasn't important in that moment. And someday we might discuss whether a mirror can reflect itself. Surely two mirrors can reflect one another. And I have learned that by exchange of ideas two people can reflect one another, even when one of the people is very young.

Home Education Magazine, September/October 1999

The bio that was with that one:

Sandra Dodd's children are Kirby (13), Marty (10) and Holly (7), who have helped inspire her to encourage frustrated moms everywhere to lighten up, slow down, and be *with* their children. They live in Albuquerque, New Mexico, in a house full of everyday treasures.

Holly was older when she asked the Zen question,
but younger when she first pondered mirrors

If You Cannot Avoid Standardized Tests...
...then just invalidate the results.

Here is a short piece from the February 2000 issue of Home Education Magazine's online newsletter. They unfairly called this "Sandra Dodd Cheats on Tests." I never did! I'm simply and subversively recommending that in the absence of the opportunity to avoid them altogether, the second best option might be invalidating them. (The paragraph beneath appeared in the newsletter too.)

On the topic of testing: I have a very serious suggestion, which will seem like a joke, but I'm absolutely soberly recommending this:

Cheat.

Don't cheat to get a better score or a worse score. Just invalidate the test either by taking too long, or making a pattern with all the answer marks in odd-numbered sections, or using dice to decide anything for which the answer isn't absolutely obvious to the child.

If the parent and child both know in advance that the scores could not *possibly* actually begin to attempt to reflect the child's "actual" knowledge or intelligence or aptitude or value, then that number will lose its juju and its ability to harm the child-parent relationship.

Of all the things I believe strongly, one that has changed my life as profoundly as any one other belief is my personal knowledge that test scores can and do (can't fail to) affect the treatment a child receives at his parents' hands. High scores, low scores, average scores—no matter. Parents cease to treat the child as his original, known self and color him soul deep with that number.

My life would have been different. My husband's life would have been different, without those 5th and 8th grade ITBS scores. I venture to say without even knowing who is reading this that your life would have been different, and specifically I believe your life would have been better, had not you been branded with a number on your "permanent record" (there's a big mean scary joke, the "permanence" and important parts) as a young innocent ten or thirteen year old full of potential, at some unknown point on a learning curve which might soon be at its settled-out point, or might just be beginning.

Why I Like Homeschooling in New Mexico

I have been privileged to be in contact with homeschoolers all over the place, including just about all of the U.S., Canada, Japan, Australia and New Zealand. I've been thrilled by the opportunity to speak at conference in Texas, Ohio, California, and this summer I'm speaking in Nevada.

I want to be in *none* of those places, though, longer than a visit. I want to be in New Mexico, and here are some of my reasons:

The weather is wonderful. Even when it's way too hot, it's not Phoenix-hot or Houston-hot. When it's too cold, it's not Minneapolis-cold.

It's not crowded. There are fewer people in the whole state than in most major cities, and so you're very likely to run into the same families over and over, and your kids won't feel so lonely. Museums and movies and stores aren't packed to overflowing with other bodies. There's room to wiggle and run.

We have mountains, deserts, and rivers. We can be at the Rio Grande or in the mountains (not at the same time...[2]) within fifteen minutes. Much of New Mexico has water opportunity and scenic opportunity at least close enough that you could get there by lunchtime and have a picnic.

Cute little trees and plants grow everywhere. In the mountains, *big* trees and ferns even, in the Jemez and some other places. Even our stickers are kinda cute—goat heads are like medieval caltrops. Tumbleweeds are very picturesque (when we're in the car and they're outside). Cockleburrs—cute name, cute plants, cute stickers, hard to get out of the dog's tail, though.

Good kid food. Tortillas with melted cheese—you get your quick food *and* cultural awareness all in one. Add refried beans and some ground beef and lettuce and you're hugely in the Mexican cooking business (for kids anyway). Mac's Steak in the Rough; Blake's; Garcia's; Garduño's. I'm happy.

Friendly peace and quiet. With some low rider and construction exceptions, being out in public in New Mexico seems way more peaceful than I've experienced in other locations. People are friendly and they wave and smile and talk.

Interesting history is all around. We forget to look at things that tourists come long ways to see. Anytime we have the urge for input from the pre-Columbian

---

[2] So said I when I wrote it, but I was writing in Albuquerque and I will note here that the Rio Grande north of Velarde kinda qualifies as mountainous. And by "we" I meant residents of Albuquerque. I grew up in Española, and used to resent Albuquerque's royal "We," but now having lived in "the big city" so long, I understand it. Apologies to all those New Mexicans who can't get to the Rio Grade in fifteen minutes, or to mountains either.

Indian cultures, the Renaissance explorers, the Wild West, the Civil War, territorial and early statehood buildings and stories and sites. . . there they are, everywhere. The mining museum at Madrid, Bandelier, the Palace of the Governors, Old Town in Albuquerque, Coronado State Monument, Los Golondrinas, the site of San Gabriel near San Juan Pueblo—and that's just the big stuff between my house and my sister's!

My friends are here. I have lots of wonderful friends from La Leche League, from when my kids were babies; from homeschooling (still collecting those friends!), from the Society for Creative Anachronism (which New Mexico does exceptionally well), and I have some friendly neighbors. I like the people at the grocery store. I like the people at the bookstores. I *like* the people here.

The dress code is lax. I was in court the other day to be a witness (two drunks got in a tussle and my friend Cathyn and I broke it up). Lawyers weren't all doodied up. Long-haired male lawyers, flat shoes on female lawyers. Young, female judge. People dressed casually (except that one teenager in a full suit who must have done something terrible to be so dressed up). People can go to Popejoy or to the opera in jeans and t-shirts and nobody has a fit. The performers are more important than the audience. My kids can wear funky used clothes and still have tons of friends and social opportunity.

This has nothing to do with homeschooling except for the "everything" part. Living in such a fine place makes it easy for families to be happy and for children to learn with joy and confidence and pleasant feedback from others.

People don't have to drive new cars. In some states, either the presence of automobile manufacturing plants or rust factors (wet places) or emissions strictures (California) make it hard or illegal to drive old cool cars (or affordable, merry clunkers). New Mexico is a car show every day. A pickup in every yard!

Secrecy. I always loved kid-novels with secret rooms, secret passages, hidden staircases, false panels—and New Mexico is almost like a giant secret room. There are people in Texas who've never heard of it. Maps mix it up with Arizona. Even the $3 t-shirts at Walgreen's with "NEW MEXICO" emblazoned across the front show armadillos and sequoia cactus, neither of which is local at all. We are, in part, secret and invisible. How cool!

Peace, love, warm tortillas, deserts and mountains to all of *Enchanted Families'* readers!

Enchanted Families, Summer, 2000

The Adventures of Holly Dodd in East Yorkshire

Miss Holly Dodd, eight years old, of Albuquerque, New Mexico, spent three weeks in Kirk Ella, a small, obscure little town near Hull (which is a large obscure town near York) in England this June. She was accompanied by her mother, Sandra Dodd. They were visiting Mr. and Mrs. Leon McNeill, usually of Albuquerque, who are living in Hull while Helene McNeill (the mom) studies medieval history and archeology. Holly went to visit her longtime friend Jasmine McNeill, formerly a student at Monte Vista Elementary.

Holly visited St. Andrew's School in Kirk Ella, which Jasmine attends, on three different days. She wore a uniform as the other children did. These were three of out of four of Holly's only days in school thusfar, counting half a day once visiting Monte Vista.

While in England Holly was also (politely) accosted on a street corner and in a playground by girls about her age asking her *very* many questions: "Where do you go to school?" was always the first one, followed by "Where are you from?" Then they would go back to "What do you mean you don't go to school!?"

As we weren't in London or another touristy town, it was apparent that we were foreigners, and Holly was often interviewed intensely. Other parents told her and me, "Oh, homeschooling isn't legal here." I know for a fact it is, I could have quoted their laws and given them a website and a mailing list to join, but I opted to say true but less intrusive things such as "Well it is, but not so many people are doing it here yet." I was on vacation and not on duty as a homeschooling missionary as I so often feel myself to be here, so I gave the short answers.

To make the vacation restful and fun for an eight-year-old (as we were the only two of the family who went), one of our main activities was going to markets, which included car boot sales. Different towns and neighborhoods have different "market days," and these markets are quite a bit like the flea market at the state fair grounds, but with meat and fish being auctioned, and lots of fruit and vegetable sales. That's the market end of it. Then there is "the car boot"—boot being our "trunk"—and people set up tables and sell their junk.

Holly learned the money more quickly than I did, and she could understand people's accents more quickly and easily too. We were there three weekends, and so in addition to the money she had saved up, she was getting her allowance in pounds (four pounds making the six dollars she usually gets), and at the end of the trip she still had money.

Junk in one country is not the same as junk in another. Some of this stuff was wonderful. We learned as much from asking people "What is this for?" as we learned from all the tourist brochures and booklets and historic sites we saw. We heard people's accents when they weren't being tour guides or otherwise working with the touristing public. We saw people interacting with their children in very everyday ways and places. We ate local food. Yorkshire pudding isn't pudding in any way whatsoever (by our standards)—and it's something pretty wonderful. We saw a Yorkshire terrier in Yorkshire. We ate crumpets and clotted cream.

Holly wasn't interested in the minsters or cathedrals or the castles. She tolerated some touristing and didn't whine about museums much, but when I saw the extent of her boredom I changed plans. I could have pressed her to look at things she didn't understand, but I've been there before and have seen those things. I needed to spend time with Holly at her level more than I needed to see yet another whatever-it-would-be.

Flash back to late April, weeks before we left on the trip: Holly said, "Mom, is *Cats* still at the theatre?" meaning live to see, somewhere.

I said, "I think it's closing in New York in a few months. It will only be in London then."

Holly looked at me politely and said (as politely), "London, *England*?"

Slowly it occurred to me that I had failed to consider one of the best things about going to England—taking a *Cats* fan to see *Cats*. So our one expensive plan was to see *Cats*, and we did. We got to sit in the second row at the matinee the day before we left, and it was just about indescribably glorious. If any of you get to London and get to see this, just do it. You will not be sorry. Even if you have no idea what *Cats* is about, go. Holly will tell you all about it before you go if you want an intro and a "*Cats* appreciation" preparatory.[3]

We stayed long enough in Kirk Ella to see the same people twice, to go to our favorite places a second time, and for Holly to get to know some of the girls from the school. She and Jasmine spent the night at the home of a girl whose father is from Scotland and whose mother is Malaysian, and they all went to the circus, and to a swimming pool, both of which were exotically different enough from American pools and circuses that she was thrilled and will remember for a long time. The girls found a hedgehog crossing the road, and they took it home and fed it and put it in a safer place. *Holly adds later that she got to take a tick off a hedgehog; that doesn't happen to everyone.*

When Holly was unable to get into a pub after 9:00 to hear an Irish band (friends of our hostess), the band agreed to come to the house for their next rehearsal and so Holly got to watch them close up. English homes are small, and we opened the drapes to watch Holly and Jasmine dance in the garden to the live pipes and tinwhistles and drums.

I'm glad we had friends living in England and I'm grateful that my husband was willing to stay home while Holly and I spent some of his hard-earned money. I'm

---

[3] The very long run of *Cats* in London closed a couple of years after our visit.

glad our housemate Wendy was able to stay home with Holly's brothers so I didn't have to worry about them. I'm glad I knew enough to compromise with Holly on activities instead of trying to drag her through all the things I would have liked to have done and seen had I been traveling alone or with an adult or teen. We were a team, and were on vacation together. Because we stayed in Kirk Ella, it was more like she actually lived in England for a short time rather than zipping through looking out the windows of tour buses or staying in various different hotels.

When I was her age I had been from west Texas all the way to New Mexico, and that was it. When I was twice her age I had added Colorado and California to my world. Holly has been in eighteen states or so, Canada and now England. I'm thrilled to be able to give her more than I had as a child, and to give her the real world instead of schoolbook peeks into the real world. I hadn't even seen Carlsbad Caverns until I was grown, and we had (and visited) relatives in Carlsbad!

On behalf of the child I was, and of others like me, I would like to ask you all to slow down and think of what your child hasn't seen and might like to see. Within your means and schedule, what can you do with and for them that will open the world up? Have they seen the Rio Grande from somewhere besides a car window on a bridge? Have they camped in the Jemez? Have they been to Santa Fe by more than one route? Have they been to Bandelier? White Sands? Coronado State Monument? A prairie dog town in a vacant lot on Juan Tabo? I recommend a child's-eye-view vacation.

I trust we will have many more adventures in years to come, even if we never leave Bernalillo County. The best thing about the trip to England was the closeness and love between my sweet daughter and me. I'm glad we went, and I'm glad to be home. I'm glad to be with Holly.

Enchanted Families, Fall 2000

Magical Thinking and Spoiled Children

I won't build up to the punchline: I don't believe money makes kids spoiled, and I don't think they will be spoiled by getting their way about things.

It seems to me after all these years of hanging around discussions of whether it hurts to give kids what they want, that "spoiled" is a boogey man parents use to scare one another and themselves. From observation and nosiness/curiosity and teaching, I've gathered a lab sample of lots and lots of families. I truly believe that very much of such behavior is genetic. And with that proposal there comes the modeling problem—nature or nurture?

"Spoiled" has more to do with a bad attitude than with privilege and wealth (of stuff, or of attention, or of money). Selfishness and casual cruelty and thoughtlessness are the marks of being spoiled, whether a child has stuff or not. When a poor child is that way, people say "Well what do you really expect? Poor kid has nothing." When a rich child is that way, they say "OH, it's directly attributable to all that *stuff* he has."

So parents who have traditionally wanted justification for treating children "like children" (seen and not heard, told to wait until they're older, told things are none of their business) jump on this accepted social truth and use it as an excuse when they tell their kids "NO!" They disguise "no" as a kindness. "I don't want you to become a spoiled brat." Or they say "You're only asking for this because I bought you something last year, so now I'm sorry I ever bought you anything," and soon the insults are fast and furiously eroding trust and respect.

It is possible for a parent to do more damage by giving something and then taking it back than by never giving anything at all. We know a kid with a sweet but poor dad and step-mom, and a more affluent real mom. She gives him *cool* stuff–a guitar, a car–but then doesn't let him have them or use them for all kinds of minor offenses. She sold something he had (I forget what) because he was "bad," and she sold it without his approval–just sold it to strangers to teach him a lesson. The lesson he learned was his mom is not a reliable or fair person, and he rendered the car unsellable with a bat or a sledgehammer or something, just in case she was planning to benefit from taking that one back too. And she says he's a bad, bad boy. Only at her house, it seems.

So the attitude and intent seem more important than the dollar value or the mass of stuff.

Holly, who just turned nine, gets an allowance of 75 cents per year of age, so she was, up to last week, getting $6 a week. Now $6.75.

We took her to Disneyland. She had saved all her birthday gift money (which amounted to about $35 from her grandmothers and her brother), and her allowance for several weeks, and she had loaned me $20 a few months before and

63

said "Keep it for Disneyland." She had $104, some in cash and some in "the bank of dad."

She came back from three days at Disneyland with $84 and a cute safari hat.

Nobody discouraged her from spending her money. She just doesn't *need* anything, because she gets lots of things when she wants them, and so she doesn't have that desperation to acquire.

Kirby, at 14, gets $10.50 a week and he has a job that earns him $30 a week or sometimes a bit more.

He bought one Mad Hatter hat and a little skull of Elvis (which he calls "the skull of pharaoh" after the pharaoh in *Joseph and the Amazing Technicolor Dreamcoat*) to use as a table marker for a game called *7th Sea*.

Marty was practically penniless. We kept offering to buy him something if he really wanted something. He finally got a skull (without pompadour) for a game marker, and a pirate scarf with Mickey Mouse ears (which he's sharing with me). I think they knew if they had wanted something–a toy or a t-shirt or whatever–that they could have had it. So their decisions were not made on any basis except "Do I really want this? Would it make my life better to have it?"

When a child is needy, he's rarely needy of things. He wants proof of regard and affection but he might not know that. If his life needs to be made better, he'll try whatever he can (until he gives up trusting and trying).

I have known children with nearly nothing who suffer preventive deprivation by parents who don't want to spoil them, who are bullies away from home and always clamor to have their way, to be first, to have more. I have known children who are given their way, an opportunity to be first, and more than they ask for, and they are fine with going second, with sharing, or with giving up the best seat to someone who just really wants it.

There is no magical prevention for bad attitude, but if parents are modeling a bad attitude with their own unreasonable selfishness or arbitrary system of denying children, they should expect their children to show arbitrary selfishness to others.

If you've never thought of these things, please consider them. If you find yourself thinking or saying anything like "You think you're entitled to things" or "You're so full of yourself," please consider the effect this will have on the image a child has of himself. Children *are* entitled to love, protection, and positive experiences within the parent's means. They *should* be full of self awareness and self regard.

"You can't give what you don't have," some people say, and if you want your children to give generosity and kindness and patience to others, you should give them so much they're overflowing with it.

Enchanted Families, Winter 2000

Art, Aging and Spirituality
Connections between Things and Ideas

The editor gave me a list of three topics, and a happy memory of 9th grade English came to me—some of us used to take the list of ten vocabulary words, the directions for which were "use each word in a sentence," and try to use them all in one sentence. Sometimes we'd need two or three sentences, but we considered those who wrote ten different sentences to be missing all the fun. Remembering that reminds me of how long I've considered words some of the finest construction toys around. When I've taught people about the history of English, I've used the analogy that Anglo Saxon words are like blocks (put together but still separate, like upkeep and downtown and playlike and upside down), but words we have from French and Latin are tinkertoys with attachments that don't stand alone (interesting and fascinating combinations of exceedingly complicated construction). That was thirty years ago—in the late 60's and early 70'—that I was so newly interested in rolling in words.

In 1970 I lived in Hokona Zia dorm, at UNM. I was 17 whole years old, and had my mom's old 1952 Singer portable sewing machine. India-print bedspreads were $4 and $5 each at Gold Street Circus, a hippie shop that wasn't on Gold Street, but on Central across from Hodgin Hall. (Now it's the west end of Bike World.) Up

Central at Wellesley, where a restaurant named Kelly's lately opened, there was a Goodwill. It had been a car dealership way before I was born. You could still tell by the building where the office, the repair shop, and the showroom had been. I bought two garments for a dollar apiece, and copied them many times. Between that and a little book called *The Illustrated Hassle-Free Make Your Own Clothes Book*, I grew brave about sewing without bought patterns.

Most of my India-print clothing was worn happily to rags. But one little yellow, brown and green flower-patterned shirt, based on one of the little tops from Goodwill, was in great shape and waiting in a box of old clothes for its unforeseen adventures.

I waited to have children, and my youngest is nine now. She came upon this hippie-shirt and wanted to wear it. I have seen her on Central, and at the University, in that top which has been there before. As with every single other place and person, some things at UNM are the same, and some are very different.

Holly has become fascinated by musicals. When I was her age I knew nothing but *Peter Pan*, from TV. She can do some detailed comparison/contrast on *Jesus Christ, Superstar* and *Godspell*, and can sing *Joseph and the Amazing Technicolor Dreamcoat* through with feeling. All of those date to the time of that shirt, of my learning to sew, of my word-rolling, and of my philosophical blossoming.

I was studying education in the early 1970's, having wanted to be a teacher since first grade. The university was a hotbed of radical new thought about learning, spirituality, the value and valuing of the human life and spirit. I was in my late teens, and eager to take my turn at trying to change the world. We read all the then-current discussions of classroom failure—James Herndon, A.S.Neill, Jonathan Kozol and John Holt—and I lived and breathed in their hopeful vision of the future of free schools and open classrooms. I taught hard, and after six years I quit. I never did quit learning, though.

Newer John Holt books were waiting for me fifteen years later, when my firstborn son was expressing his distaste for organized activities and formal learning.

While I was making him little medieval costumes and taking him to feasts and tournaments where I set him down to play with his collection of could-have-been-medieval wooden and clay and metal toys, he being part and parcel of that ongoing work of performance art which is the Society for Creative Anachronism, I started to think that maybe school wasn't going to benefit a child who was resistant to group control and already surrounded by learning opportunities of which my distant impersonal gurus of education would have approved. Homeschooling seemed part and parcel of the respect for individuals and the attachment parenting which had flowed so freely from my previous experiences.

We all are preparing for our unseen futures, and I was prepared to homeschool. I am prepared to discuss the social history of the 70's musicals Holly is frolicking with now, in a shirt I made when a brand new India print bedspread could be bought by a barefooted hippie for $4. She is surprisingly prepared, at the age of nine, to understand it.

Enchanted Families, Spring 2001

Unschooling: You'll See It When you Believe It

Following years of sporadic reports by people who claimed they had tried unschooling but it hadn't worked for them, I started tracking their similarities and, as usual, I learned something new. And, as usual, I thought I should share it so others might not have to wonder for ten years.

So here is a snapshot of what I thought I knew when I sat down to write this one day not too long ago: Some people don't know what unschooling is supposed to look like.

If I went to the flea market to buy a torque wrench but I didn't know what one looked like, I would have a pretty hard time just finding one by looking around. It probably wouldn't be on a table with clocks made of cross-cut cedar. Looking through a tray of cassette tapes wouldn't help. It would be especially difficult if I didn't even know what a torque wrench was for. I might look all through those wirey-boards and steel boxes computer-repair guys brought. I could look for hours through cloth and paperback books and come home saying "Going to the flea market for a torque wrench doesn't work."

I used to go to the flea market regularly, pre-motherhood, to buy medieval- and Renaissance-suggesting things to re-sell in the SCA. It was fun. I used to make enough to pay our way to tournaments by setting up my little homemade tent and some tables covered with pewter and silver-plated bowls and plates, cast aluminum tankards or goblets, hand-blown glasses from Mexico, fur collars, little wooden jewelry chests, old-looking jewelry, leather bags, brocade curtains (without fiberglass or rubber), interesting little knives, wooden trays and bowls, and so forth. I'd sell them cheap, too. I learned a lot doing that, and had fun.

The Albuquerque flea market is huge. I would stand, walk, and pull my cart for two or three hours, scanning for shiny metal dishes, wood, leather, certain designs. But most of the stuff got only enough glance to determine it was NOT what I was looking for. I ignored piles of baby clothes, electronics, plastics and hand tools. Many a torque wrench lay unseen.

Unschoolers come away from a small school and into the big wide world. Some say "Here is the wide world, and we will be in it and learn from everything around us." Then they proceed to scan specifically for math, history, science, reading and writing. Because they went to school, math to them looks like flat paper with numbers on it. History looks like books: many words and a few maps and illustrations, all arranged in chronological order. Science is wide open—it might be a microscope, or a bug cage or some rocks and a magnifying glass, until the kids are older, and then it will start looking like numbers on flat paper, or maybe a book on anatomy, or the feared and revered "Periodic Chart of the Elements." Reading and writing should look like reading and writing have always looked— books without illustrations (eventually, and the sooner and thicker the better), and reports with straight margins and numbered pages.

They scan their children's lives every day for schoolish things. They're looking for spiral notebooks and they ignore sunsets. Looking for a 50-minute session of history to prove attention span, they miss a pioneer dress-up game and an attempt to build a catapult.

As a final stop before giving up, some come and declare their failure to those who told them about unschooling. They tell us it didn't work for their family, and that after all, they are the experts in their children, and so they know that their own family is not creative enough to unschool, and their children crave structure. Sometimes it seems they think those who say "Unschooling is So COOL!" are deluded nuts who don't care much about their children. Other times I think they see our children as brilliant and theirs as dullards.

Now I have come to believe that they just ignored the million things looking for the five or six.

They thought if they left the kid alone for a month he might spontaneously create a four-subject routine, with some music, art and sports put in for extra-curricular balance. They envisioned that their child might say, at the age of fourteen (give or take a few) years, "I'm ready to learn biology now," which would be the beginning of nine months of study, with three dissections and some tadpole measuring, maybe some plant genetics. By May he should have declared whether he was more interested in botany or life sciences (step one in "do you want to go to medical school?").

When a science-minded kid loves to take the dog down by the river and look for wild berries and snakes, some parents say, "My kid just wants to play. He's not interested in learning. He'll never learn science just playing."

Each little experience, every idea, is helping your child build his internal model of the universe. He will not have the government-recommended blueprint for the internal model of the universe, which can look surprisingly like a school, and a political science class, a small flat map of the huge spherical world, a job with increasing vacations leading to retirement, and not a lot more.

Unschooled children can organize their knowledge in free and better ways. They never need to feel they are through learning, or past the point that they can begin something new. Each thing they discover can be useful eventually. If we help provide them with ever-changing opportunities to see, hear, smell, taste, feel, move and discuss, what they know will exceed in breadth and depth what any school's curriculum would have covered. It won't be the same set of materials—it will be clearer and larger but different.

"How will they learn everything they need to know?"

Do the best of the high school graduates know everything they need to know? No, and at some point, ideally, they start learning on their own. Some fail to get to that point, though. Unschooled kids have a head start. They know how to find what they need to know, and they have not been trained to ignore things that won't be on the test.

When parents see how and what their children are actually learning instead of just scanning for the half dozen school-things, unschooling will make sense to the parents. If you wait for school to congeal from a busy life, you'll keep being disappointed. If you learn to see everything instead of just school things, unschooling will start working for you. When you see it you will believe it.

Home Education Magazine, November/December 2001

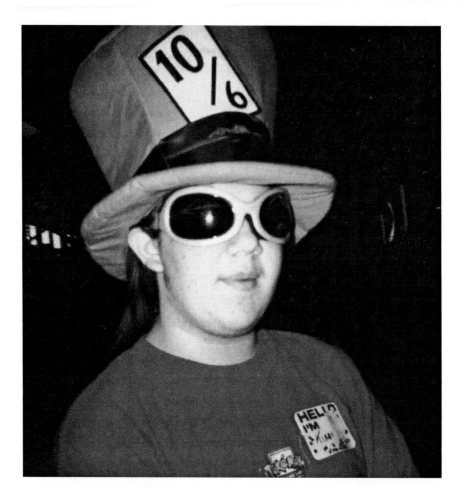

King's X From the Math Monster

"What about times tables?"

The fascination some parents have with the magical power of knowing times tables amazes me each time I hear that question.

I stopped counting up around the fiftieth time.

"Do your kids do times tables?"

What does "do" mean in relation to a table? Discover it? Too late. Write one out? This "table" of which they speak is a block of data, a pattern of numbers, involving relationship and function. What's to do? It's done.

My kids can "do it."

What my kids can't do is to answer speed quizzes like "What is six times nine?"

Meanwhile, they can calculate 6% (local sales tax) and 30% (the discount Kirby gets on gaming supplies) in their heads. Once a much younger Kirby wanted to walk to the corner store for a Dr Pepper. He asked what he could do to earn money. I whipped up a blank table with 1-9 across and 1-9 down, showed him what the multiplicatory deal was, and said I'd give him a penny a square.

"How much money will that be?"

"Same as the answer in this square," and I indicated the 9x9 square.

Marty was only four or five, but he wanted in on this money-making puzzle, so I made him one too.

They helped each other, filled theirs in, figured who was right when there were discrepancies, *loved* finding the patterns, and nearly forgot about the sodas.

When they got back from the store (with change, as it hadn't occurred to them to stop when they had reached the price of the soda), they were still excited about that chart.

We had a big new concrete patio, and one night the whole family and some friends were playing outside. When a spinning, jump-roping, free-for-all game got old and they were tired, I chalked out a chart about 8 feet square, and the kids started filling in the easy parts—2's, 5's... soon there were only six or seven squares left, like 7x8 and other intuition-avoiding combos.

I have never before or since seen such total *doing* of times tables.

Jody Hegener once told me a tale of having been challenged by kids from a Waldorf school who waited until they had an eleven or twelve year old Jody headed out on horseback at a ranch with them to ask the big question: "Do you know your times tables?"

Jody told them she didn't know if she did or not, since she didn't know what "times tables" meant.

Ooh, they had her good. But they told her what it was that she knew so little about, and they demonstrated, zipping on up to the times twelve they knew (way better than the nine or ten limit of public schools).

So Jody was up with them and getting the pattern on the elevens and twelves, and said "What about 13?"

They didn't have to know 13. It wasn't so fun anymore. Jody told me she was multiplying by 14 when they finally got her to stop. I imagine she was thinking of how very easy fifteens would be.

But "times fifteen" won't be on the test.

This summer Kirby was overheard explaining to some other teens at the gaming shop how to multiply by 18. Do it by 20, and subtract two for each one you have. No pencil, no paper, and the school-labeled "learning disadvantaged" friend totally understood.

The adults who overheard this expressed amazement.

The other homeschoolers who heard about it were amazed that adults had been amazed.

Perhaps knowing the times tables, "doing" the times tables, is a magic safety from further math trauma. "I know my times tables" is like "King's X" from being tagged by the math monster. My kids think math is a tool and a toy and a game. Why would they want to be saved from it?

"We don't have to know that" isn't anything I have ever heard my children say. Because there is nothing they –do- "have to learn," there is nothing that is off their learning list either . In artistic terms, without the object there is no field. In math-lingo, they have the infinite universal set. In a philosophical light, they avoid the dualism of learning and not-learning.

If you are new to math in the wild, I have some recommendations of things that worked well for us. First, don't be teacherly about any of this. Don't use the talking-to-a-poodle voice (and if you don't have one or don't know what I'm talking about, GOOD!).

72

Then, gradually gather some subset of this sort of math stuff, plus other things it might remind you of:

*two or more matching **geoboards** and colored rubber bands (you could get just one, but then you can't copy each other's designs):

***pattern blocks**, even if your kids are older (we have the wooden ones with the yellow hexagons being the biggest), because there are angles to mess with and because they're very soothing

***Cuisenaire rods** if you can get them for less than full price (or if you're rich), but don't worry about the "real exercises"

*Yahtzee, Bazaar, Master Mind for Kids (cuter, friendlier, simpler version than adult Master Mind), playing cards, poker chips (not necessarily for playing poker, just for messing around with, making patterns), and Clue (Kirby says there is a new D&D Clue game out. We have the Simpsons version.)

*real **money** to spend

*computer and video **games** like Zoombinis, KidPix, Harvest Moon, Mario, Link & Zelda

*don't discourage **Magic**, Pokemon or other "CCG's" (collectible card games); D&D and other dice games involve much math and strategy

The other day in my kitchen I said, "Hey, Kirby, I might make $100 for an article on you teaching someone to multiply by 18, and you didn't even know I overheard you talking about it, so I'll give you $10."

"Cool. 10%. I'm like an agent or something."

His 23-yr-old first-time visitor got big eyes and said, "You were teaching someone to multiply by 18?!"

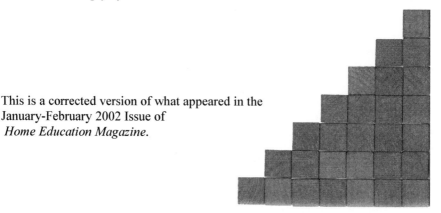

This is a corrected version of what appeared in the January-February 2002 Issue of
Home Education Magazine.

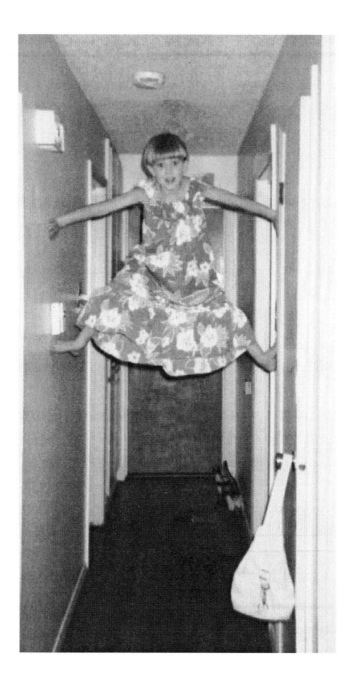

How Holly Takes the World for Granted

There is a photo of me, with a column I wrote, in the November/December issue of HEM. Holly, at nine, took the photo. She took lots of me, with a disposable camera, in a little wooded place of her choosing. She picked her favorites, and we sent them in.

So I took the just-arrived issue to her and showed her the cover, and then page 56, and said "Look! They used one of the pictures you took!"

She looked at it, looked at me, smiled (somewhere between wanly and half-heartedly) and said "Cool! Thanks for showing me that." And she went back to the pattern-puzzle she was working in her lap (one of those with the cars, I think—Rush Hour) and to the TV show she was watching.

Okay then.

Being published in an international magazine doesn't thrill her. It still thrills me when my name's in the fine print in a regional newsletter, so maybe I know how big the world is and she (at nine) doesn't. Or maybe I'm more easily thrilled.

But I think Holly takes the world for granted. And why not? The world is hers.

The world wasn't mine when I was little. It belonged to grownups, and I was told how to sit, what to say, what to eat and how to hold the spoon. I was told where to play, who with, and how long. If I got dirty or tore my clothes I was in trouble. I was told what was good and what was bad.

Holly takes the world for granted, and I'm thrilled about that.

One of my online friends, Anne Ohman, wrote this and gave me permission to quote it: "I know that when I sat in a Catholic church and the priest asked me to repeat *Lord, I am not Worthy to Receive You...*, I knew it wasn't My Truth. I *had* to believe I was worthy...even though this was the message I was receiving everywhere...home, school, church...I just *had* to hold onto the tiniest glimmer of Hope that I *was* worthy of the beautiful gifts of Life."

I remember once I was a teenager, walking with several friends of mine, going north on Lower San Pedro Road, which parallels the Rio Grande in Espanola. We were walking slowly, playing with sticks and rocks. I don't remember what the subject matter was, but I said "I wonder how they do it in the REAL world." One of them said, "This IS the real world."

I didn't quite believe it.

There I was with Jon Tsosie, from Santa Clara Pueblo, across the river; and DiAna Trujillo, whose dad was in the Bataan death march (yet living up the road); and I think John DePaula was there that day, whose dad was from Queens, NY, and whose mom was from Trinidad, Colorado; maybe another kid or two. I thought the real world was far from us—that we were spectators and marginal not-even characters.

Maybe I thought that if you were good in school, you could grow up and become a real adult with a job. And if you were good in New Mexico, you could grow up and move to a more real place. But somehow I had the idea that "real" was elsewhere. And "important" was not me.

In the years since then I've slowly grown to have a much different point of view. But in Holly, when I showed her that picture, I saw that she doesn't worship "elsewhere" and she doesn't envy "other." She feels as real and as right as rain. "As right as rain." A natural, worthwhile, real part of everything around her.

My friend Mark grew up in North Dakota, and his relatives were of German farming families. They were Lutheran. There was no nonsense. The way that Mark was put in his small place was that he was told, "You are full of yourself." It wasn't said in a positive or a good way. It was intended to be a deflating insult. Mark doesn't have children, but we've talked a lot about being and having children. He likes that my children are full of themselves, and full of the whole world.

Sometimes I'm jealous. Sometimes I think that it's a bad thing that Holly wasn't thrilled about being published. Then I think that maybe the main reason I am giddy at the idea of having my words in print is that it is evidence of reality. It means I am up and out of school, and I am no longer just in New Mexico. And then that awareness brings me full circle. Holly will not have to overcome the fear that she is unworthy.

I remember one of the icons of hippiedom, the Desiderata. It said, "You are a child of the universe, no less than the trees and the stars." That was a radical thought in the 1960's, for some people. Belonging naturally to all that's around you. Being as solid and as real as a tree.

This is what unschooling, though, has done for Holly. She is not a student. She is Holly. She is not a fourth grader. She is Holly Dodd. She has been since birth, and she will be until or unless she decides to go by another name, but that will be her decision. The world is hers in a way that the world has never been mine, not even now as an adult. Sometimes I see myself as a messy amalgamation of experiences, certificates, test scores and labels, just come lately into the real world.

I see my children living full, real lives today, right now. I don't see them as students in preparation for life, who after a number of years and lessons might be considered "completed" or "graduated." It was a long way to come, and I never even had to move. I just had to look at what I considered to be real.

The Desiderata was written by Max Erhmann, and for those who missed it then or had it then and have missed it since, here it is:

Desiderata

Go placidly amid the noise and haste, and remember what peace there may be in silence. As far as possible without surrender be on good terms with all persons. Speak your truth quietly and clearly and listen to others, even the dull and ignorant; they too have their story.

Avoid loud and aggressive persons; they are vexations to the spirit. If you compare yourself with others, you may become vain and bitter, for always there will be greater and lesser persons than yourself. Enjoy your achievements as well as your plans.

Keep interested in your own career, however humble; it is a real possession in the changing fortunes of time. Exercise caution in your business affairs, for the world is full of trickery. But let this not blind you to what virtue there is; many persons strive for high ideals, and everywhere life is full of heroism.

Be yourself. Especially, do not feign affection. Neither be cynical about love; for in the face of all aridity and disenchantment it is perennial as the grass.

Take kindly the counsel of the years, gracefully surrendering the things of youth. Nurture strength of spirit to shield you in sudden misfortune. But do not distress yourself with imaginings. Many fears are born of fatigue and loneliness. Beyond a wholesome discipline, be gentle with yourself.

You are a child of the universe, no less than the trees and the stars. You have a right to be here. And whether or not it is clear to you, no doubt the universe is unfolding as it should.

Therefore be at peace with God, whatever you conceive God to be; and whatever your labors and aspirations, in the noisy confusion of life keep peace with your soul.

With all its sham, drudgery, and broken dreams, it is still a beautiful world. Be cheerful. Strive to be happy.

by Max Erhmann, 1927
(The Desiderata is public domain.)

Article, including Desiderata, appeared in *Home Education Magazine*, March/April 2002

Late-Night Learning

I don't know whether it's the dark or the quiet or biological cycle, but many of our family's best stories begin "One night…"

Once when Kirby was little, I was reading him to sleep with *What Your First Grader Needs to Know*, and he got so excited about the definitions of music that he got up to go tell his dad that music has melody and rhythm. He was clapping a pattern I had shown him. His dad, having been a musical guy since childhood, wasn't surprised at the news, but he WAS glad that a five year old could be so interested.

Just lately we've had a couple of tales worth telling. It was about sunset when Holly came and asked me what a Sousaphone was. I said it was like a tuba, but re-arranged so people could carry it, kind of wearing it, while they marched. While I was looking for a photo of one, I told her it was developed by John Phillip Sousa for marching bands and that some are made of a white plastic sometimes these days, but were always brass at first.

I asked why she was wondering about Sousaphones. She said that on Barney (*Barney & Friends*, on PBS), a guy who works at the school had one.

I looked in the encyclopedia, and in a book on musical instruments. There were other places, in other rooms, to look (illustrated dictionaries, the internet) but we didn't leave that corner of the library where we were for the next couple of hours. I pulled down a game called "Music Maestro II," which used to be advertised a lot when I was first homeschooling, and which I had bought at a thrift store a couple of years ago for $2.99 but had never yet opened. I hoped for a Sousaphone, but it didn't have one. It had cards with lots of other instruments pictured, though, and a cassette tape with samples of the sounds. Holly wanted me to play that right away.

I thought any moment she'd lose interest. We went through the modern instruments tape, putting the cards in their proper spots on the game board, or diagram, or whatever it could be considered. The game has older instruments mixed in with newer ones (Renaissance instruments set in among modern orchestral instruments), and Holly is familiar with recorders and lutes. So when the first tape ended and hadn't gone through all the instruments, she wanted the second tape.

During this, we had remembered to look in the *Musical Instruments* volume of the Scholastic First Discovery series, those with the plastic-overlay pages, and it did have a Sousaphone.

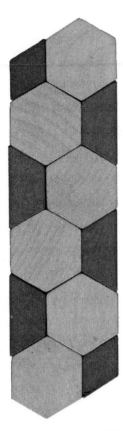

Holly ended up leaving before the second tape ended, because something more interesting came up. But by that time we had been playing with musical ideas and pictures and sounds and history until well after dark.

One night Holly had been working with marionettes she was making out of cardboard tubes, string and dowels. She came where I was online, reading, and asked me what the "car" was in "cartoons"–what did the word really mean? (While fact-checking this article for me Holly said she asked because on a commercial they had said "car keys, carTOONS.")

I looked in the dictionary and it seemed from the etymology that it had to do with the pasteboard (called "cartone" in Italian) used for models for paintings in the Renaissance. I thought maybe they were sketching miniatures of paintings. I pulled out a piece of tagboard from my paper-stash, to show Holly what thickness "pasteboard" might have been, because they weren't using corrugated cardboard, for sure.

My husband, Keith, passed by and heard us discussing this idea, and said he had just lately seen a special on PBS about transferring sketches to other surfaces and that the tagboard "cartoons" were full size, kind of like stencils, with holes through for transferring the details.

It was great that while we were trying to figure it out from a dictionary, along came someone who lately saw televised explanations of the methods of 500 years ago. Keith was saying, excitedly, that they were discussing fresco paintings, and that that's the way Leonardo da Vinci had transferred the designs to the ceiling of the Sistine Chapel.

"Michelangelo." That was Kirby, from his bedroom next door. "Michelangelo did the Sistine Chapel."

"Oh, you're right," said Keith, the dad.

I was most impressed by the calm joy with which this information was being exchanged. Kirby wasn't gloating that he corrected his dad. It was very matter-of-fact. Nobody was embarrassed or frustrated in any of the discussion. It could have gone longer, but we were done! It was great.

I can tell you part of why Kirby knew these things. For one, my sister has a full-sized rendition of the God-and-Adam elements of that painting on the inside wall over the door of her house. The house they've been building on for years has a two-story center section, and there was a big empty wall over the door. Their friend is a painter and he caused God to touch Adam again, and Kirby saw it before, during, and after. But beyond that, Kirby has always been a Teenage Mutant Ninja Turtles fan, and sought out information about the artists they were named for when he was just a little guy.

It seems lately that more and more people want to know exactly *how* to unschool, but the answer is not what they expect. Looking back at these stories, in light of others like them, the best recommendation I can make is to open up to the expectation of learning. It helps if the parent is willing for a conversation to last only fifteen seconds, or to go on for an hour. Remember that if your "unit study" is the universe, everything will tie in to everything else, so you don't need to categorize or be methodical to increase your understanding of the world. Each bit is added wherever it sticks, and the more you've seen and wondered and discussed, the more places you have inside for new ideas to stick. A joyful attitude is your best tool. We've found that living busy lives with the expectation that everything is educational has made each morning, afternoon and evening prime learning time.

Last night, a Sunday evening, four adults were working a jigsaw puzzle of the Kings and Queens of England, which I had bought at a charity shop in England. Elsewhere in the house, four teenaged boys were playing card games and video games. Holly, who's ten, came up into the library where the puzzle was out and said, "Can I play?"

"Sure!"

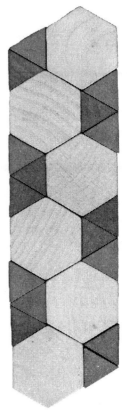

We listened to Marty Robbins' cowboy ballads, the soundtrack of *My Best Friend's Wedding*, Emmy Lou Harris duets, part of *Annie Get Your Gun*, some Weird Al, and finished a thousand-piece puzzle with text and illustrations of historic events in England from 1066 to the 1960's. Holly matter-of-factly discussed heraldry, crowns, ermine, royal succession, conflicts between France and England, and art.

The puzzle was done around midnight. My husband had quit at 10:45 to go to sleep. The adult guests went home, and I read Holly to sleep.

I don't know exactly what will be happening at our house today, or this evening, but I have every expectation there will be warmth and kindness and humor and learning.

Home Education Magazine, May 2002

Disposable Checklists for Unschoolers

Beginning homeschoolers are often afraid. Sometimes they homeschool for a while, and a curriculum keeps the fear to a manageable level. Sometimes a curriculum is a workable alternative to school for a family. For some it is not. Some of those give up and the kids go back to school. Some give up the curriculum and move toward unschooling.

Beginning unschoolers are often afraid. Without the touchstone of a schedule and a list, they don't know how they will see progress, or how they will recognize "sufficient effort" on the part of children or parents.

For some people, treating their first months of unschooling as summer vacation, or a month or two of Saturdays is sufficient, but some people schedule even their Saturdays and vacations. "Just hang out with your kids" sounds torturous to them, and may be more frightening than abandoning public school was.

Here, then, are some possible replacement checklists and scheduling aids for those who truly want to unschool but who can't breathe well or sleep soundly without a plan.

Sink-Like-a-Stone Method: Instead of skimming the surface of a subject or interest, drop anchor there for a while. If someone is interested in chess, mess with chess. Not just the game, but the structure and history of tournaments. How do chess clocks work? What is the history of the names and shapes of the playing pieces? What other board games are also traditional and which are older than chess? If you're near a games shop or a fancy gift shop, wander by and look at different chess sets on display. It will be like a teeny chess museum. The interest will either increase or burn out—don't push it past the child's interest.

When someone understands the depth and breadth of one subject, he will know that any other subject has breadth and depth.

Universe-in-a-Drop-of-Water Method: Can one intense interest come to represent or lead to all others? A mom once complained that her son was interested in nothing but World War II. There are college professors and historians who are interested in nothing but World War II. It can become a life's work. But even a passing interest can touch just about everything—geography, politics, the history and current events of Europe and parts of the Pacific, social history of the 20th century in the United States, military technology, tactics, recruitment and propaganda, poster art/production/distribution, advances in communications, transport of troops and food and supplies, espionage, prejudices, interment camps, segregation, patriotism, music, uniforms, insignia, religion....

When someone really understands one war, he can easily understand another, because he will have all the framework and questions in his mind. When he understands how countries are born, invaded, and how a government can die out, he understands truths about all nations and civilizations.

But there may be no overriding interest like chess or WWII in a child's life yet, and might rarely be. So then where do parents go with their fearful unschooling energy?

Here are some checklists to try. Mix and match them. Use them as main ingredients or as spices or occasional garnishes. Take those you like, and leave the rest.

FIVE SENSES

The obvious senses are sight and sound. Pictures of Japan and a recording of koto music might be considered sufficient for school. But how much more gloriously can you round that out when you have access to all kinds of real-world resources? Add taste, smell and touch. The kids don't need to know there was a checklist, but for the parents, a trip to a restaurant or an Asian market or gift shop might help them complete their secret framework.

How long should a five-senses checklist take to finish? Since unschooling operates in the real world, timing it to an hour or a week or six weeks is artificial. No hurry to "complete the set" on something. Smelling an elephant might need to wait for a trip to a zoo or circus, or you might want to just avoid that particular scent sensation altogether.

TIMELINE

A smaller list with a larger effect is to consider the past, present and future of a topic or item. "Ancient Egypt" is sometimes considered in a glossed-over, snapshot kind of way, but even that spans thousands of years. What was in the Nile Valley before the civilizations we know about? What's there now? What might be there someday? These things can be brought up casually, without appearing to be the checklist they are.

When were the first electric guitars made? What's better about new ones than those made forty years ago? What might be the future of electric guitars?

GEOGRAPHY

Lists are patterns. Lists can take the form of grids, and so a pattern-loving parent might use the globe or a map as a checklist. Where are the fewest traffic lights in your state? This came up at our house last month—we heard that Harding County, in northeastern New Mexico, has not one single traffic light. So we looked on road maps, and population maps, and couldn't help but see which counties have lots of towns and highway intersections. We thought there might be other states that have a county with no signals, or maybe more than one county. Some states probably don't. Some states don't even have counties.

Which continents have the most traffic signals? Butterflies? Poisonous spiders? Which have the least, or none? If the Nile Valley is the site of the oldest advanced civilization in its region, where are the oldest known civilizations on other continents? What is the oldest continuously inhabited spot near you? In your state? In another country you've been to or dreamed of seeing? The histories of Constantinople, Rome, Paris and London are easily accessible and illuminating. What geographical factors caused people to settle there so long ago? What did Alexander the Great find when he marched east?

FANTASY, REALITY AND MYTH

What aspect of some particular subject involves objective truth? What is folklore or mythology? What literature or fantasy has come about based on that subject or item? Consider dragons, or India, or snakes, or rainbows. Checklist Abe Lincoln, the discovery of fire, or the depths of Lake Superior. Plot WWII, Japan, electric guitars, or Egypt.

A professor once told me in all seriousness that the universe is as infinite inside our heads as it is outside. I thought he was goofy. But as I've gotten older and my personal model of the universe has continued to expand, I've come to understand what he meant. Inside, each of us is building an internal "map" or grid of information. The more bits and pieces we have, the easier it is to connect them. School tries to build the same structure in all students, or at least tries to supply them with a set of matching parts sufficient to build a rudimentary model of the universe, but each student ends up creating and working off his own map.

Unschooling allows free use of any and all bits of information, not just school's small set. A grid based first on cartoon characters or the history of ice skating can be expanded just as well as one built on a second-grade version of the discovery of North America and the made-up characters in some beginning-reader series. If the goal is to know everything, and if each person's internal "universe" is unique, then the order in which the information is acquired isn't as important as the ease and joy with which it is absorbed.

The time will come in your unschooling when you will forget to use checklists, but it won't matter. The child's internal grid will already have given him the need to know how things feel, smell and taste, and what they used to be or will be, and whether it's different in other places. Connections will continue to be made throughout his life. The universe inside will grow larger and the universe outside will become clearer with every new experience.

Home Education Magazine, June/July 2002
Canterbury Home Educators, Term 3, 2003 (New Zealand)

Marty at Disneyland, and skating at a neighborhood park
in Minneapolis, where ice grows wild.

Deschooling for Parents

Once upon a time a confident and experienced scholar went to the best Zen teacher he knew, to apply to be his student. The master offered tea, and he held out his cup. While the student recited his knowledge and cataloged his accomplishments to date, the master poured slowly. The bragging continued, and the pouring continued, until the student was getting a lapful of tea, and said, "My cup is full!" The master smiled and said, "Yes, it is. And until you empty yourself of what you think you know, you won't be able to learn."

Weird Al says it a different way in "Everything You Know is Wrong," and Christians say "You must surrender yourself." Before that Jesus said, "Unless you become as a little child…"

What it means in homeschooling terms is that as long as you think you can control and add to what you already know, it will be hard to come to unschooling. The more quickly you empty your cup and open yourself to new ideas uncritically, the sooner you will see natural learning blossom.

So much for philosophy and buildup. How can this be done? Can it work for former teachers? What about engineers who are sure their children need lots of math in an organized fashion? What about moms who love schedules and organization?

Deschooling is needed much more by parents than by children. I still have subconscious school-stuff to slough off; it surfaces when I least expect it and I wrestle it, encapsulate it, and try to forget it.

Here's a way to schedule some deschooling and avoid the time-wasting stress of trying to build unschooling out of school-parts.

Quick Installation for Unschooling: Just stop.

Stop thinking schoolishly. Stop acting teacherishly. Stop talking about learning as though it's separate from life.

Gradual Installation (necessary in most school-trained cases):

• Think about everything you've ever learned. Make a list if you want. Count changing the oil in your truck, or in your deep fryer. Count using a calculator or a sewing machine. Count bike riding and bird watching. Count belching at will and spinning with your eyes closed if you want to. Think about what was fun to learn and what you learned outside of school.

• Watch some or all of these movies. If they make you think of any other movies you haven't seen for a while, or never got to see before, watch those too. But watch these, with or without kids:

Mary Poppins
Heidi (with Shirley Temple)
The Sound of Music
Searching for Bobby Fischer
Ferris Bueller's Day Off

You don't need to think too hard about those movies. No tests, analysis or reports. Just let the images and ideas flow through and over you. Come back to them after a while, when you've been unschooling a while.

• Remember school. Take a breath and picture your favorite, clearest school year. See all the elements of its form and organization. Is it vivid?

Okay. Here is how you learn *not* to overlay all that on your unschooling life where its structure and terminology will disturb the peace and hinder progress. I am asking you to take your school memories, add light, and stir.

First Phase: "Learning" replaces "teaching"

Replace any form of the verb "to teach" with "to learn." It will involve some rephrasing, and sometimes you have to back up and totally revise the statement or the idea. Replace "I taught him…" with "He learned…" Replace "I plan to teach him…" with "When he learns…" (You might want to retroactively revise your earlier thoughts too. If you think you taught your child to eat or talk or walk, you might want to replace those memories with "He learned to walk by pulling himself up and trying it," and so on.)

Advanced Phase: Speech Purge

Don't use any of these school words: semester, grade, age level, grade level, scores, subjects, school year, school hours, school day. Don't even have a school minute. And when school is gone, life will be left.

Get a coin bank or change cup or a box with a hole in it. This is important. It can be literal and earthly, or an imaginary coin bank in your head, if you're shy. If you use a school word, put a coin in your fine-bank. If you're using the word to convince yourself that unschooling isn't going to work, double the fine.

When the cup fills up, spend that money on something for you and your child. Ice cream or a movie, maybe. A slinky or a helium balloon. Not a workbook or a protractor. If a year goes by and the cup didn't fill up, take the whole family to dinner at a cool restaurant you've never been to before and celebrate!

Final Phase: Thought Purge

Fine yourself for even thinking in those school terms.

Having excised the offending concepts you will have extra room in your head and you can fill it up with your newfound unschooling awareness.

• Change your schedule. Some people like to see learning parceled out evenly over the year, over the week, or over a day. But life is lumpy. As with chaos theory, or statistics and probability, there are "busy" times and big quiet loops that seem to be going nowhere and actually have a destination. Think "leaps and bounds," with rests in between.

Instead of looking for "steady pace," look for fits and starts. What if a child has a great piano week and practices two hours a day and then he's tired of it for the rest of the month? It wouldn't all be lost and over and ruined. What if, one day, he just *gets* some mathematical concept. Will you recalibrate the level at which you want him to work steadily? Or can he take a break for a month or a year without you panicking?

Kids at school each "get" multiplication once, and after that they're just hearing the explanation over and over while the teacher rephrases and re-introduces and reviews in hopes that some of the other kids will "get it" that day.

The "steady" pace schools simulate is 1) not real, and 2) not applicable to natural learning anyway.

"Having history" 180 times a year is like trying to teach a pig to sing. In one good half an hour, an interested and curious (i.e. "ripe") child might learn as much about the Civil War or Apollo 11 as she would in a week at school (if ever). And history is all around us all the time. We're making it today.

• Look directly at your child. Practice watching your child without expectations. Try to see what he is really doing, rather than seeing what he's NOT doing. If you hold the template of "learning" up and squint through that, it will be harder for you to see clearly. Just look.

When you have completed some or most of the exercises above and you no longer tense up at the thought of whether your child could possibly get into college, and when you can hear "math worksheets" without thinking "Maybe we should get some of *those*!" you can consider yourself a graduate of Sandra Dodd's Advanced School of Deschooling.

Congratulations! Below is your combination final project and field trip:

Rent some movies and watch with your kids. Here's my recommended list, but let personal preference rule. You might have better ideas:

Spartacus
El Cid
Ben Hur
The King and I
Monty Python and the Holy Grail
   (maybe send little kids for popcorn during Castle Anthrax)
Star Wars (all)
Karate Kid (all three in marathon can be good!)
Hamlet (I like the one with Mel Gibson)
Romeo and Juliet (Zeffirelli's, from the late 60's)
Singing in the Rain
Joseph and the Amazing Technicolor Dreamcoat
O Brother, Where Art Thou?
The Music Man
Last Action Hero
Galaxy Quest
The Miracle Worker
Fly Away Home
Paper Moon (Holly's recommendation)

Discuss as little or as much as the kids seem interested in discussing. By this point you'll be past the need to wonder whether there's anything worth learning in those movies, and you'll see your kids learning and laughing and being glad you're there.

Have fun learning for the rest of your life!

Sandra Dodd, former mother of toddlers, has had three large children sneak up on her over the past ten years. They just keep hanging around the house and *learning* things.

Home Education Magazine, September/October 2002

Words, Words, Words

One of a child's best tools is to learn to ask "What's that?" It's one of a baby's keys to knowledge. "Sa-sat?" said one of my kids. Hundreds of times, pointing. "Sa-sat?" Another said, "Aht-dat?"

With names for things, categories form. Some small furry animals *are* "dog" and others are not. "Not" needs another name.

On naming, a researcher named J. Doug McGlothlin wrote, "A child possesses a natural desire to call an object by its name, and he uses that natural desire to help him learn the language. He receives real joy from just pointing out something and calling it by name. He never thinks it is stupid or silly to say something that others might consider obvious. For him, it is delightful. When Colin learned the words for star and moon, he would point them out to us at every opportunity. He could not play with them or eat them, but he loved to call them by name."

Is naming a game or is it the most profound learning of all? It's both!

One day when Kirby was a toddler, his dad said carefully and clearly, "Kirby, close the cabinet." Kirby gazed back with no understanding. Keith tried again sweetly: "Close the cabinet!" Nothing. I saw the impasse, and said quickly, "Kirby, shut the door." He lit up with recognition and *slam*, it was done.

That day, I decided to try to use more than one word when I communicated with my kids. I knew that in England, after the Norman conquest, simple legal matters had been stated in English and French both, and some of those phrases still exist, like "will and testament," "aid and abet," "give and bequeath," and "null and void." So for the sake of my children understanding both my child-of-Texans self *and* my child-of-Bostonians husband (Boston and Michigan and Canada, but *not* Texas), I began to paraphrase. "Kirby, can you hand me that blue cup? The plastic mug that's on the counter?" Or "Let's go to the park, okay? We'll walk down to the swings and picnic tables."

I didn't realize how much I was doing it, and how naturally, until I started doing it in adult conversations. So I backed off, because by then my youngest was five anyway.

When these bigger, stronger kids were playing with balls, bicycles, ramps, puzzles, building sets, tools, trees, ropes, their own gymnastic abilities, there wasn't so much to talk about. "What's that?" wasn't their first question, but "Can I go try?"

In review or analysis of those projects, new words certainly came up. The great thing was we were naming things they had already mastered or begun to understand, in discussing why something worked well, or didn't, or why a ball thrown fast against the wall could come back and hit you really hard. And so we came to words about physics, and force, and vectors, pulleys, gears, and materials. Anatomy lessons came free with sprains, scrapes and bruises. Biology just bubbled up when stickers or insects or rusty nails punctured skin. In the course of answering questions and trying to explain what went wrong or what might work better, we used new words. Science lessons for their own sake, or vocabulary lists, would have done little good (and some harm) but naming what they had already done, felt, tried and accomplished was just a bigger-kid's "What's that?"

As they got older, and war games, movies about history, and international celebrities came over their intellectual horizon, so did trivia about the borders of countries. What's with Tibet? Taiwan? When did Italy and France settle into their current borders? Why does Monaco have royalty? The Vatican really has cash machines in Latin? What's the difference between UK and Great Britain? Is Mexico in North or Central America? Were Americans *really* that afraid of and ignorant about the Soviet Union in the 60's? In answering those questions, the terms and trivia of history, geography, philosophy, religion and political science come out. The words are immediately useful, and tied to ideas and pictures and knowledge the child has already absorbed, awaiting just the name, or the definitions, or the categories.

"Grasp the subject, the words will follow," said Cato the Elder (234 AD - 149 BC), who wouldn't have been able to use the cash machines at the Vatican even though Latin was his native language. My kids could show him by gestures how to use the terminal, though, while he read the choices, if he showed up today with an ATM card.

The tests homeschoolers sometimes worry about are given in words: GED, ACT, SAT—all vocabulary. Even the math section is done largely in words. So realizing that words are the everyday tools we use to discuss swordmaking and sourdough starter and torque wrenches, our quickest path to a rich vocabulary and all the concepts that go with that might be to discuss history, make bread and fix our cars with our children.

I'm happy to know I'm not the sole source of information for my kids.

Last night I came to use my computer and there was a dialog on the desktop, a leftover instant message between my thirteen-year-old son Marty and an older homeschooler. This was the entirety of that dialog:

Marty: You coming down?
Other kid: yeah.
Marty: Did you know Canada has Prime Ministers?
Other kid: yeah
Marty: dude

Now I will never have to explain to Marty that Canada has a prime minister. I don't know why he cared, on a Friday night in New Mexico, but it doesn't matter.

The playground of words is humor. I don't discourage my children from Monty Python, George Carlin, Weird Al Yankovic, and other linguistic athletes of that ilk. Laughter and commentary about people doing circus tricks with words is a world above and beyond vocabulary lists. I do recall, though, my friends and I made even vocabulary lists fun when I was in school by trying to put all the words in one or two sentences, or by using the words as words, like "The word 'obfuscate' is rarely used," or "'Discrete' is a homonym of 'discreet'," without any hint we knew how to use the words in context (which we usually did).

One of those schoolfriends from that same English class is one of the best dads I know. His name is Frank Aon, and he lives in Santa Fe. I was asking him one day about having young children when many of our friends are grandparents. Frank waited even longer than I did to have children. He said, "I wanted to wait until I felt [I was] safe to have kids…to be a father with presence, mindful in word and action. I get to watch them change from tiny little beings to adults, if I survive and if they survive, so each moment of interaction is precious."

"Mindful in word," he had said, which reminds me that words have the liberating power to bring order to the universe, but they also have the power to harm, to limit and to sadden. So be careful with words. Use the good ones, the happy ones. Play safely out there!

Now I will document the name of this little word-frolic. It is from a sort of instant message between Hamlet and Polonius, who might have been his father-in-law if things had gone differently:

> Lord Polonius: What do you read, my lord?
> Hamlet: Words, words, words.
> Lord Polonius: What is the matter, my lord?
> Hamlet: Between who?
> Lord Polonius: I mean, the matter that you read, my lord.
> (Hamlet II, ii, 191-195)

Mel Gibson did that scene on Sesame Street a few years ago, with Elmo. My kids got the joke, which was proof they knew something of Shakespeare. One of the greatest benefits of knowledge is that one gets jokes.

And so having already quoted a Roman historian and William Shakespeare, let me close with a Greek wordsmith who loaned his name to a Simpsons character:

> "There is a time for many words, and there is also a time for sleep."
> Homer (~700 BC)

Home Education Magazine, November/December 2002

How to Raise a Respected Child

Holly says the ice cream we have in the freezer is too sweet. She had chocolate milk last night and said there was too much chocolate in it, so she divided it and made chocolate milk for someone else with half of it. She usually prefers plain milk.

Plain milk tastes *way* better if it's your choice than it does when it's plain because someone else wouldn't let you put chocolate in it.

Without free choice, how can a person choose what is plain and good?

Unschooling begins with a choice between going to school or not. How many millions of people are never given that choice?

Next is the choice between "doing school-work" or not. Sometimes new unschooling parents are hoping that holding their breath and waiting might lead to children studying a curriculum, just as the mathematically-allegorical monkeys might type *Hamlet*.

In the success-bearing phase, unschoolers stop looking for *Hamlet* or even for English history. But knowing that Ian Holm, who plays Bilbo, plays Polonius with Glenn Close in a Mel Gibson movie causes it to be worth a look for lots of people. And he was Fluellen in Kenneth Branagh's *Henry V*, too. If they watch *Hamlet* or *Henry V* because of *Lord of the Rings*, is that like chocolate milk, or like plain milk? If they don't watch *Hamlet* yet, or ever, that's fine too.

The most peaceful unschooling families have loosed the ropes that held learning at the dock. They have developed faith in the idea that humans learn best in freedom.

Perhaps it's just a pretty truism, about unschooling families. Maybe it is as real as granite. Here are some other patterns for your consideration, though: Unschooling families with young children often fear for the neighbors to "test them" and find them wild or "behind." Unschooling families with older children politely try to hide their smugness at the positive responses of others to their older unschoolers. How does that change come about?

There are traditional dialogs adults have with stranger-children. They ask what school they go to. They ask whether the child likes his teacher, and what his favorite subject is. My children haven't gotten past the first two questions, because if "I don't go to school" doesn't stump the interviewer, "I don't have a teacher" usually does. And so an adult who succeeds in having a conversation with an unschooled child finds himself speaking with a person, and not "a student," not "a child."

For some, this is their first real conversation with a person who isn't grown to adulthood. My kids are used to being the first, in that way. They're used to the look in people's eyes when they realize that here is a child who has something to talk about and who will confidently and guilelessly speak.

How does that confidence arise?

I really believe unschooling works best when parents trust a child's personhood, his intelligence, his instincts, his potential to be mature and calm. Take any of that away, and the child becomes smaller and powerless to some degree.

Give them power and respect, and they become respected and powerful.

Is it just that simple? That a parent can *give* a child power and respect? Can a parent give a child freedom?

With the freedom to choose what they eat, my children have bypassed sweets more times than I could have counted, and eaten hearty, real food. I saw those choices working before they were old enough to go to school, or not to go to school. They had all the food they wanted.

With the freedom to choose to stay up or to go to bed, I saw toddlers ask to go to bed because they were tired, and then saw them go to sleep smiling, and wake up happy. They had all the waking they wanted, and all the sleep they wanted, instead of feeling deprived of either.

Of my childhood, I remember tears over pancakes. EAT THEM NOW. I didn't eat them again for fifteen years, after that forced-pancake day. Was that good for nutrition? Discipline? Love? Respect? No, it was destructive. I remember being forced at school and at home to drink milk. Was one glass enough? Then is half a glass enough? Will a child drink not one drop more than he *has* to? Is milk better than peace?

For many children, information is treated like cold pancakes. Skills are forced like too-warm milk.

What if hot pancakes, served with a smile, would taste really good with milk? What magic happens when it's fully acceptable for a child to say "No thanks" to hot pancakes?

Neediness expresses itself differently with different kids.
Abundance expresses itself similarly in all.

Neediness creates various interpersonal problems, health difficulties, psychological stress and sorrow. Chronic neediness becomes a vacuum that cannot be filled.

Abundance in one person provides benefits for others. A child with all the trust he needs can trust others. A child with all the time he needs can share that time with others. One who has freedom won't begrudge freedom in others.

Most people have never known a kid who has experienced true abundance. Most have never met a child who had been given a full measure of respect, so that the child was respected (already) and full of respect (respect*ful*). It is easy to respect someone who has that respect already, and who has so much that he can spread it around to others.

An abundance of love, of confidence, of *self* and of freedom will create a flow of respect from and toward a person.

Sandra Dodd's children are Holly (11), Marty (13) and Kirby (16). They have never been to school, and they eventually came to amaze the neighbors. Their abundance is shared with others, usually in Albuquerque, New Mexico.

Home Education Magazine, January/February 2003

Geography

My husband and I were watching *The Lord of the Rings* on DVD, sitting in the glow of Peter Jackson's Mount Doom, and I said, "Tolkien obviously didn't study geology."

The mountain formation around Mordor, in the Middle-Earth maps doesn't show any regard for plate tectonics, but Tolkien wrote early, and he lived in England, and he studied languages. He's excused. The idea that Elrond and Isildur could stand on an unmelted rock ledge in the midst of a volcano and discuss whether the ring needed to go in the lava or not is more fantastic than flying Nazgul. I'm sure that later Frodo and Gollum will stand there and discuss it too, and that stone platform will *still* not have melted into the surrounding lava.

But it's only a story.

I studied geography and its related geology when I was thirteen and in a Jr. High classroom where sand came through the closed windows that had been installed by the WPA in a really cool, big adobe building, and the sand had to be blown off the pages of our four pound geography books before we could turn to the next page. This was the llano, the sand hills, half a mile west of the Rio Grande, in Española, New Mexico. I later taught English in that same room where I had learned to spell Tanganyika and Zanzibar. I later blew sand off pages of books, maybe some of the same sand I had blown out of the chapter on Peru and Lake Titicaca. We had a guest speaker during the cold war, who had been to the Soviet Union and told us about a coke machine with a public glass. When you put a coin in, the coke dispensed into a glass that people drank from and then left for the next

person. That illustrated the dangers of communism, and the superiority of our scientific knowledge and sanitation and democratic way of life.

After eighth grade, it seemed, I was going to be through with geography, done for life. I had a piece of paper with an "A" written on it that I could carry always, to excuse me from any further geographical exercises.

Two of my three children are older than thirteen now. They know about Tanzania for three or four reasons. Tanzania didn't even exist when I got that final passing grade in geography. I know about Tanganyika and Zanzibar, which quickly became history and not geography. If I were to suggest to my children that there was any difference between history and geography they would look at me as though I were speaking nonsense. Good for them. They know that the dissolution of a nation, or the creation of one nation from two, involves religion, language and culture, personal politics, support or the lack thereof of their neighboring states or sponsoring allies or colonizing powers. Nobody told me that in school. Nobody told my children that at home, either.

They know Lake Titicaca lies between Bolivia and Peru. You know how they know that? Animaniacs. A funny little Animaniacs song we have on a sing-along video.

In a conversation at a restaurant the other day, technology and warfare came up, and I ran quickly through the technological "ages" of stone, bronze, iron and steel, to make some point I was making about stone-age cultures in the 17th century, and Kirby, who's sixteen, said he knew all that. Two seconds after looking at him to see whether he was offended at my condescension or whether he was just being matter of fact, I said, "From playing *Civilization*, right?"

Right.

I still forget. After eleven years of unschooling I still forget sometimes that the information that was doled out to me on a schedule is just *out* there for my kids, that they find it interesting and that they have no reason to avoid adding it to their fascinating collection of trivia about places, people and the world around them.

One day I was on the phone to a potential local homeschooler who was agitating about whether to take a fifteen-year-old boy out of high school. I was doing my own riff on unit studies, saying some people like to do two week units, and feel they're "through with dolphins" or whatever, and I said, "But you can't finish China."

Kirby, who was sitting in the room waiting for me to give him a ride when I was off the phone, said, "The Huns tried that."

"What? OH! My son just said, 'The Huns tried that.' I didn't teach him that. He learned it from a game, or a movie, or something." Kirby gave me a look that indicated that he didn't learn it all in one place, it's just one of those truths of the universe, free for the taking.

When I was teaching seventh grade English, long ago, instead of planning a poetry unit, each Friday I gave them the lyrics to a traditional English (or Scottish, or American) ballad, and then I sang it for them and told them what I knew about it. I never did any poetical analysis, just told them "It's Friday, and we're doing ballads on Friday." This one year, I was writing the lyrics on the board, and they could copy them down. One girl said with the avoidance-voice, "Do we have to *memorize* this?"

"Nope."

Some Fridays the ballad was short and they would request that I sing one of their favorites from a previous week. Many of them would sing along. Sometimes I'd miss a Friday and they would not be happy about missing their ballad.

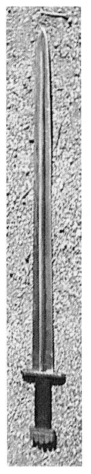

In later years when I would meet one of those former twelve- or thirteen-year-old students, the thing they would remember and mention (or sing) was almost always a ballad. What they didn't have to learn was what they will carry all their lives. One ballad was about the Crusades, and Turkey. One had a parallel Scandinavian folktale, about rape and murder, and they asked, "How could they not recognize their own brother?" so we talked about life before photographs, and the travel realities of the Middle Ages. More than one ballad involved "a little pen knife," and we talked about quill pens and homemade inks, and life before pencils and ballpoints. One was about a train wreck on a three-mile grade. I wasn't supposed to be teaching history, folklore or science. But there was geography in all that bygone life, in stories handed down through generations.

The world is all a-swirl with music and maps and photographs of interesting architecture, costumes and ancient weaponry and technology. Gypsy carts and camel caravans and steam loco-motives have their places on the planet, and nobody has to memorize anything to sort them out into their times and cultures.

So how do unschoolers learn geography? Better than I did in school. They learn it with flexibility and a lack of awareness of having "learned geography." They learn it from games, movies, satellite photographs, globes, the history of ships and airplanes, of cloth and houses, of Okinawan karate and of Roman bathhouses. Their model of the universe is better than mine was when I was their age. Their confidence is better than mine is now! They are learning about *their* planet. I felt like an unwelcome guest here, when I was "just a kid." They feel like natural residents of Earth, and they do know their neighborhood.

Home Education Magazine, March/April 2003

Typical Unschooling Day

People ask the hardest questions sometimes. One of the hardest to answer is "Can you describe a typical unschooling day?"

Sometimes I've said "like the best Saturdays you remember from when you were a child." Some Saturdays or Sundays were taken over by relatives or emergencies or mechanical failures or illness. Those days happen, when the sun seems to go down before people get to do what they had planned. And some days are just too perfect to tell, for fear of intimidating the audience with a fluke of an incredibly rich, productive and photogenic day.

I would like to recount an actual recent incident, and how a string of events led up to an unschooling day.

Three years or so ago I bought a book of biographies of U.S. presidents. It's been here and there in the house, but a few months ago it was in the kitchen. Marty picked it up and commented that some presidents only had half a page. And some had funny names he had never heard, like "Millard Fillmore."

The book came to be leaning on the side of the stairs up to the library, for re-shelving. Weeks passed.

Last fall, totally unrelated to the book on presidents, I ordered a presidential timeline poster from C-Span. Someone online had mentioned that it was available free to teachers, so I ordered one, took a look, and left it on my desk. Time passed.

At Thanksgiving dinner at the in-laws', I mentioned the chart. I was the only one in the family who had seen it. The wall it would fit on already had some Christmas cards up. I wasn't in a hurry anyway (which was good, because I had a broken leg).

One day in February, Holly said "We should play Encore." Encore is a singing and trivia game we bought at a thrift store long ago and have played lots. Teams try to sing phrases from songs containing a certain word or topic, like "cars," or the word "little." Holly said, "We should sing songs about presidents. I know three!"

Other than the vague thought that somewhere in the Disney song "Davy Crocket" a president might have been named, I couldn't think of one.

I need to back up about twelve hours. I had read myself to sleep with an article on *The Simpsons* in which the author wrote, "There are reasons why the U.S. Poet Laureate, Billy Collins, told me *The Simpsons* is 'the only reason I own a TV'." And the morning after that (the morning of the typical day) Holly had said,

"Names on *The Simpsons* are really different. Like 'Milhous'." I had told her that was the middle name of Richard Milhous Nixon, who was president not so long ago.

So to win her round of "Encore," Holly said she could cite the Animaniacs song on the presidents, and one from *The Simpsons* called "We are the Mediocre Presidents." Marty came in just as Holly was singing "Oh do you know George Washington," to the tune of "The Muffin Man."

"That's not a song," said Holly's worldly, song-filled fourteen-year-old brother.

"Yes it is. It's on a tape at Genna Miura's house!"

Okay. Holly three points. Me, Marty and Davy Crockett, zero.

Holly went back to singing "We are the Mediocre Presidents" and I said, "Marty says that in that book on presidents, some just have half a page. They might be the same guys."

Holly got the book to see if it could be a simple truth that some presidents had only been half-page presidents.

"FDR. Is he the guy in *Annie*?"

"Yes." (Holly's favorite historical period is the Great Depression. She likes the music, the clothes, and the stories of hardship and social change.)

"This guy looks like he's from Texas."

"Lyndon Johnson was the only one really from Texas," I said, and then muttered a bit about George Bush Sr. and trailed off saying I guess maybe George W. might be an actual Texan. Holly wasn't listening anymore. She was looking at a cartoon illustration of Theodore Roosevelt. He's the one she had thought looked like a Texan, from the picture. I checked the fine print for her.

"Oh! Born in New York City, but he was into horses and such."

While I was scanning for information on whether he had lived in the western U.S., to help him be more like a Texan for Holly's sake, I read aloud that he was the first president to do some very notable things:
    first to ride in a plane
    first to travel outside the U.S. as president
    first to ride in an automobile

"Wow. That's a lot of firsts!"

When was he president? The book didn't say.

TIME TO UNVEIL THE C-SPAN CHART!

Marty helped me tape it up. Holly and Marty started figuring out how to interpret the graph, what the blocks of color indicated, how easily you could tell who was president when each other president was born, who had and hadn't been in the military, who had been legislators and governors.

Kirby heard them and came out to see what the excitement was. I just kept doing what I was doing across the wall in the kitchen, knowing Marty was fully capable of answering any questions Holly might have about the chart.

Holly said, "Can we leave this up until tomorrow so I can answer questions about my birthday?"

Oh yeah! That's where this started. Holly had made a beard of the cut off rim of a paper plate, put it on herself and said, "I'm Abraham Lincoln. My birthday is tomorrow."

But that's not where it started. It started because she was reading the calendar to me and asked what "A-D-H-A" spelled. I said it wasn't a word. She said it *had* to be a word, because it was on the calendar. I said "Well it's not an *English* word." It was hours later when I went and read "(Eid) al Adha." Someday I'll look it up and tell her what it is, but I didn't know myself, and the river flowed on. We'll pass that point again next February, or sooner.

Later in the day Marty was back at the chart, and declared that Reagan had been a bum, but George Bush was *not* a bum. I went to see upon what this "bum" rating was being based. The chart easily showed that Reagan was much older than Bush when they both joined the military at the same time. I ran my finger across the whole chart to show Marty that John F. Kennedy, Richard Nixon and Gerald Ford had all joined then too. Dwight Eisenhower and Lyndon Johnson were already in. What was the big occasion? Marty ran his finger back up to the pictures and dates. World War II. Both his grandfathers had joined too. Most of the young men in the country had joined.

Holly's interest in music from *The Simpsons* led Marty to a profound realization about WWII. I wasn't surprised. I didn't plan it, but I was open to it and I expect other connections and discoveries of a similar nature to happen three or four times this week.

So "a typical unschooling day" for us involves connections being made to things someone learned an hour or a week or many seasons before. That chart of presidents will be referred to and remembered for years, even after it's no longer on the wall.

In the whole unfolding, a Simpsons song Holly learned from a CD was no more or less valuable than a book about presidents, or a free wall chart from C-Span, or knowing that the story of the musical *Annie* is set during the Depression when Franklin Roosevelt (not Theodore, who's not from Texas) was president.

It all came together to help Holly build the structure to which she will tie in future bits about not just American presidents, but all other connections historical, geographical, political and social.

My children have never asked, "Do we have to learn this?" They don't have to learn anything. So everything is equally fun for them. The joy of unexpected discovery is the substance of a typical unschooling day.

Home Education Magazine, May/June 2003

Books and Saxophones

I went to school. Most people reading this probably went to school. But most people reading this probably are not sending their children to school. Many of you are probably finding that your vision of homeschooling isn't exactly the same as the reality of your child's life at home. I know my own vision missed coming true.

The nest I built for my children even before I knew we would homeschool was made of toys and books, music and videos, and a yard without stickers. It was a good nest.

When our oldest was five and our third was still inside me, we stuck our toes in the homeschooling waters, and asked ourselves some serious questions. We bypassed the regular serious questions. We weren't worried about socialization. We weren't worried about times tables. What my husband and I asked when our should-we-do-this eyes met was "What about marching band?"

Years have passed, in that sneaky way years pass. Sometimes we're so busy we look up from our work and play and find we don't know what month it is. Kids bump their heads and elbows on things because they don't realize how big they're getting. My husband and I will say "Wasn't it last year?" and Holly, our time-keeper, will say "That was three years ago in March, when Gina was here and the couch was over there," or some other clear, visual and correct reference.

So what went wrong?

I saw what I had loved as a child and I thought my kids would love that too. At first I "saw" school. I loved school. But Kirby wasn't cut out for being stuck in a school. Maybe I hadn't been either, but I had just drawn in my head and my elbows and made myself fit. And I had found happiness there.

School wasn't going to work, for Kirby at least. But still, his dad and I knew what he would love: books and music. He would have time to read all the books in the world, and he wouldn't be limited in the time he would have to learn music. What a wonderful life he could have, even without marching band.

Those thoughts took just seconds, because the reality involved bicycles and Ninja Turtles and friends and food and medieval costumes and road trips and board games.

A few years ago I reviewed my progress and realized that my three lovely children who are busy every single day and who can converse about any subject neither read books for fun much nor do they play any band instruments whatsoever.

I played clarinet from the time I was eleven. So did my cousin Nada, who lived with us. My little sister played flute when she hit the magic "age" of fifth grade. My younger cousin, Nadine, who lived with us, who was in the same grade as my sister, made a shocking choice. While student-model clarinets and flutes were around $120 each, she made a fateful declaration: "I want to play saxophone."

Saxophones cost three times as much as the daintier things the rest of us were playing. My parents didn't want to say, "No, play something smaller, and made of resin if possible, not five pounds of brass." Well, I'm sure they *wanted* to say that, but rather than seem discouraging they made those heavy saxophone payments.

In the jumble of reviewing the what and why of school and comparing our unfolding homeschooling outcomes, I learned about myself and school. "Well, of course you did," you might say, and you might roll your eyes. But wait until I tell you what I learned.

For me, band was what books were: escape.

By "escape" I don't mean escape into a fantasy world and another plane of thought. Sure, that happens sometimes with music, and more often with adventure stories and mysteries. I mean physical, outathere escape.

Elementary school band got one out of the classroom. Every hour spent in band was an hour I was not dealing with textbooks and notebooks. We were still sitting in rows, but they were high-class semi-circular rows around a conductor. I had seen orchestras do that. We were doing something adults did!

And when I wasn't in band, I used my other escape ladder, and that involved the library, extra-credit reading, and books sneaked under my desk. I had allies. Sometimes the librarian would ask me to come and help her. YES!! Virtue *and* escape. Sometimes I would be reading something wonderful under my desk that took me out of the room, out of the school and out of my skin. But it didn't take me out of the teacher's line of vision. So sympathetic friends would do a noble thing. When the teacher called my name to read aloud from the history book or "reader" that was being dragged out into the air paragraph by paragraph, I would look up shocked at my surroundings, and then glance at where someone was casually pointing at a paragraph, behind the back of the kid in front, and I would read my section as calmly and clearly as though I had been attentive. Then back into the real book I went.

We have books in our home that our children have glanced at wanly and that's about it. We bought Henry Treece books, when we saw we had boys. They are wonderful, out of print kids' novels about Vikings and Saxons. An attempt to read one aloud to Marty failed. Other nudges in that direction have been ignored. They have much better ways to internalize Vikings and Saxons than to read a novelization of something that didn't happen anyway. They have a medieval studies club as part of their lives, and great Eyewitness and Usborne books with photographs and archeological reports and maps and diagrams. Why would they want to read 180 pages of unillustrated text when their dad has a reproduction Viking sword as real (and almost as heavy) as a saxophone?

A younger Kirby tried to play clarinet, when we begged and jollied. Twice he went to the beginning homeschool band sessions, with his new reed and the old clarinet his dad still had, who had spent large chunks of life playing clarinet, oboe and bassoon in the steady pursuit of excellence at getting out of the classroom. But in Kirby's case, when he was at band he was missing something better elsewhere. His choices are richer and more varied.

Years passed. Holly is playing fiddle, and starting to mess with recorder (which her dad and I play regularly) because Cyndi Lauper played one on a concert video. We just borrowed a banjo for Marty who has said "banjo" for years, because of Steve Martin. Kirby has talked about piano, but is a busy, happy guy and it hasn't yet happened. They all sing for fun (and well).

I don't mind that my vision failed. The realities of longterm natural learning were not within the scope of my beginning-homeschooler imagination. If their lives had unfolded as I had predicted they would have been smaller and sadder. I'm very happy to report that their real, natural, unschooled lives are both bigger and happier than my imagination.

Home Education Magazine, July/August 2003

UPDATE THREE MONTHS LATER

I reported to unschoolers online that Marty was reading a book called *The Road to Miklagaard* by Henry Treece, and someone wrote "Sandra, weren't those the books you mentioned in your last HEM column as just sitting on the shelf? You never know..."

Until she wrote that, I hadn't remembered. But he didn't get it off the shelf, he found it in a little pile of stuff a moving-away adult friend had brought back to us. It was left out in the living room, and Marty saw the book and started reading it.

I had forgotten to strew!! I told him we had several more books by that author, also about Vikings and Saxons. "We do!? Cool!" So thanks, Pam T., for pointing this "update" out to me.

August 15, 2003, update on column written in May

Persephonics

"How would people know how to pronounce 'Persephone'?" Holly asked, in the car one day.

"They would have to have heard it first. Why?"

"Because on Arthur, they were doing a parody of Harry Potter, and instead of 'Hermione,' they used 'Persephone.'"

"Ah. Same deal. Unless you're familiar with the name, there's no good way to know how it would be pronounced. They're both Greek names."

I remember reading comics, and pronouncing "Yosemite Sam" YOZEmight Sam, when I was eleven or twelve years old. That reasoning followed on knowing the words "nose" and "rose," and knowing two meanings for "mite." A widow in the Bible had a mite, and the birds' nest on my porch had mites. None of that knowledge was helpful in the face of Yosemite Sam.

Growing up, I knew no late readers who weren't filled with loathing of the idea of reading. When I taught it was the same way. Nonreaders at the level I taught were filled with fear and shame. Unschoolers have been a whole new kind of people for me. My three children were later-than-school readers, but the advantage they had was that when they were decoding the written word, they had thousands more terms, names and place names to draw on than I had when I was learning, or even than I had had at their age. Because we weren't limiting them to materials "at grade level," they had been surrounded by "hard words" in real discussions and movies. They had been read to not just from classic bedtime reading and storybooks, but from magazine articles and online sources not designed for easy reading or children's supposed limitations.

I couldn't have predicted how easy it would be for them to learn to read starting with huge vocabularies, and without pressure and tests and measures. When they could read, they knew it because they started reading. The symbols turned to language. When I started reading my vocabulary was very small, and the books we were reading didn't help that. I couldn't read anything outside of that first grade "reader," but the teacher told me I was reading.

Most people have never known a later reader who was bright and confident. I hadn't before I met unschoolers. Three fifths of my family now consists of people whose late reading was not detrimental, and I have made the acquaintance of many others like them.

English has one word that, unfortunately, helps charge this whole subject with emotion and doom. I learned this from an exchange with Marty, when he was four. I wrote it down at the time, and have quoted it a few times since, but I've never connected it with reading until now.

Wed, Jul 28, 1993

> *The first thing [Marty] said after "good morning" was "Mom, if you count to infinity, is it illegal?"*
>
> *I explained to him about infinity, with a million plus one and a "gadillion" plus one. He was fine with the explanation, and I said, "Who told you you can't count to infinity?" He said I did, so I explained the difference in things that are impossible and things that are illegal (have consequences).*

"Can't" sounds pretty permanent. We were careful not to say, in our kids' hearing "Marty can't read." We would cheerfully say, "Marty doesn't read yet" (or Kirby, or Holly). With that, every time it was discussed we were clearly indicating that we thought the child *would* read before long, and it was not a concern. They were certainly learning in many other ways, as anyone close enough to discuss their reading could see!

We've used the same angle with food. "Marty doesn't like spinach yet" leaves the spinach gateway open. "Holly doesn't eat much meat" is better than "Holly's practically a vegetarian."

Recently, Kirby tested for and earned a brown belt at the karate dojo he attends. A week before, we were all discussing it in the kitchen. I said some schools will give black belts pretty quickly, but Kirby's school doesn't give black belts to anyone under 18. Holly asked how long it takes an adult to get a brown belt. "However long it takes," said Kirby.

Keith, my husband, who had studied Shorin Ryu karate as an adult for a few years said, "I certainly never got there."

"Never?" said Holly, "or haven't yet?"

Keith smiled and said, "Haven't yet. You're right. That's a better answer."

In school it can be hard to learn without reading, or at least hard to do the worksheets and answer the questions at the ends of the chapters. Learning is not such a separate thing at school.

With unschooling, I was surprised and joyous to learn that there are some things that are easier to learn without reading. I know that I myself am note-dependent. I looked through three piles of paper for the notes I took after the brown belt conversation so I could quote it exactly here. My children haven't developed that dependency.

Holly showed us twice that she could best readers in real-life situations. Once was in a play, when she learned her lines right away, since she was unable to read the script in rehearsals. By the performance, some of the readers still didn't know their own lines, while Holly knew the whole play. The other was a girl scout presentation in which all the other girls read from prepared "speeches" while Holly discussed her topic with me at home until she knew enough to stand up and speak about it. Holly was the only one who made eye contact with the audience. She was the only one who would have been able to answer questions. The girl assigned to tell us about Juliet Lowe didn't even know how to pronounce "Juliet Lowe" when she came to it on her own prepared "speech."

Holly is reading children's novels now, though, and enjoying them. She reads words on labels and boxes and signs just by glancing at them. She's eleven. She's not "behind" for her age. She been getting to this point gradually since birth, but luckily her learning wasn't put on hold until she could read!'

Her question about "Persephone" was easy for me to answer. The more of a language a person has heard and understood, the easier reading will be. The more stories they know, the more places, people and things of which they're aware, the easier it will be to recognize their names. The more words they know the easier it will be to deduce successfully words for which sounding out is an imperfect method, such as "soldier" or "machine" or "thought."

I have come to believe that parents will be happier if they read to their children, talk about the world around them, watch movies together and discuss poetry or song lyrics than if they spend that same time on phonics instruction. Whether the primary goal is learning or reading, it seems that vocabulary and understanding are of much greater benefit than knowing which vowel does the talking, especially since that rule doesn't even work for its own verb "does."

Phonics is not a magic decoder ring. It has been said by many craftsmen that you know you're *really* advanced when you find the need to build your own tools. My children are really advanced readers, because each has created his or her own set of tools. They have discovered the patterns which phonics attempts to describe, and they understand them probably better than anyone who has memorized them as lists of "rules," because they know when they work and when they don't work. In many cases they know *why* a word is spelled as it is, as they're learning the history of English as they learn to read, and they find it all as fascinating as anything else they have learned.

There's that root of "phonics" right in "Persephone." "Persevere," people say. Often they are grown before they discover that "persevere" is pronounced differently by English speakers in other parts of the world.

Where learning is concerned, it's never too late and everything counts.

A shorter version appeared in
Home Education Magazine, September/October 2003

Some Thoughts about Homeschooling

"Where do you go to school?"

"I don't go to school."

Ten years ago, that unexpected response to the typical "dialog" between an adult and a child was shocking, and stumped the questioner. Now many say, "Oh, you're homeschooled? My sister/cousin/neighbor homeschools."

For years adults have had a traditional "conversation" with new children they meet. The adult script is: What's your name? Where do you go to school? Do you like your teacher? What's your favorite subject? The child's responses varied, but never mattered. Past that there wasn't much to say. Friendly adults might have said "I like your hat," or "Your dress is cute."

That was okay, though, as children were fast being conditioned not to talk to adults anyway, but to stick with children their own age.

What happened to us!? School.

But many things have changed, and when enough things are new and different, the old ways lose their grip and we can flutter up and away.

I was asked in public once, "Are you willing to risk your children's future on your 'theories'?"

"Yes. Aren't you?" was my answer then and still is. Each parent risks his child's future on his theories. Some think very little before deciding to go with the theory that school is a necessity.

Though most people have now heard of homeschooling, there are few who know personally a child who has never been in school at all. Those I know best are my own children. Kirby is seventeen, works at a gaming shop and studies karate. Marty is fourteen, is considering becoming a policeman, and runs a weekly field-game he's designed called "ork ball." Holly is eleven, with a keen eye for mixing used clothes in interesting ways, and an ear for playing with words and music. We know many others like them. Some are grown now.

Though homeschooling is becoming more common, it is still confusing to outsiders. That's understandable, as it can be quite confusing from the inside. Hoping to lessen that confusion for readers I thought through several paths I could take: political, historical, categorical, social, practical....

For the readership of this magazine, I have decided to go with something you might not find anywhere else, and that is to tell you how homeschooling will change the world.

115

I went to school all through the 1960's, a time considered the heyday of the American education system by some. I liked school. I did well. They taught me "the scientific method" three different times, and it made sense to me. When I grew up and became a teacher, I realized that the school system is one big experiment, with no control group whatsoever. Everyone was part of the changing set of methods and measures, but there was no group that was NOT being subjected to the newest theories and methods.

In those days, the late 60's and early 70's, there were several bright, energetic school reformers, but the sparkliest was John Holt. In education classes, we were assigned to read what John Holt thought was wrong with the schools. He said that sitting in rows taking notes was no way to learn. I sat in my desk and took notes about his theories and findings. The irony lit up the room, but those lights dim easily. All around me, in New Mexico, schools were gearing up for "The Open Classroom," an idea touted by many reformers. In alternative schools and in lab schools (schools run by university education departments, for the children of faculty and employees) open classroom experiments had worked remarkably well! In regular classrooms, though, it fell apart. There were several causes for the failures, but the chiefest turned out to be that it only works when children have a choice about whether to be there. Compulsory attendance itself works against joyful learning.

That joy and force don't coexist should not have surprised anyone, but life zoomed on and there was no quiet place in which professionals could rest and observe. There were quiet places, though, where hippies and liberals of the 1970's could be, and there they went. In communes and other small communities, and in individual families who were experimenting with alternative lifestyles, homeschooling came to be. John Holt had given up on school reform by the mid 1970's and was recommending that families just keep their children home. In those writings, he coined the term "unschooling." With a book and a newsletter, he brought these unschooling families into contact with one another, and gave them hope and encouragement. The book was *Teach Your Own* and the periodical was *Growing Without Schooling*.

Around 1980, a separate homeschooling movement started among the Christian right. It was more organized and focused and involved money, with its desire and market for Christian-based educational materials.

There are no reliable statistics on how many people homeschool. Anyone who says he has them is bluffing. Every state and province is different. Some don't even require registration. Two of the largest jurisdictions, California and Texas, have very different homeschooling situations, and neither can produce useable statistics. A curriculum company could tell you how many people bought their materials, but they don't know how many tried them for a week and set them aside in frustration.

116

What is known is that homeschoolers as a group score high on standardized tests. Homeschoolers do well on national spelling bees and geography contests. A homeschooler in my town won a national storytelling competition this year.

Those bare facts give some general credence to the claims of homeschoolers, but will that change the world? A little.

There is a group of homeschoolers that generally tries not to test their children at all. Because a test score is never ignored, tests affect the relationship between parent and child, and many unschoolers want to preserve their child's journey to adulthood unmeasured, uncompared, and whole. It might seem crazy from the outside, but the disadvantage of testing is real.

Each tree grows from a single seed, and when a tree is growing in your yard what is the best thing you can do for it? You can nurture it and protect it, but measuring it doesn't make it grow faster. Pulling it up to see how the roots are doing has never helped a tree a bit. What helps is keeping animals from eating it or scratching its bark, making sure it has water, good soil, shade when it needs it and sun when it needs it, and letting its own growth unfold peacefully. It takes years, and you can't rush it.

So it is with children. They need to be protected from physical and emotional harm. They need to have positive regard, food, shade and sun, things to see, hear, smell, taste and touch. They need someone to answer their questions and show them the world, which is as new to them as it was to us. Their growth can't be rushed, but it can be enriched.

The structured homeschooling that involves buying a curriculum and teaching at the kitchen table on a schedule is not the control group the school system needed. Those who practice "school at home" serve to reinforce the school's claims that they could do better if they had more teachers and better equipment. When a structured family has high test scores, the schools say "SEE? We could do that too if we had one teacher per three or four students."

I have come to believe strongly that schools' goals are unreachable. School at home can be more of the same problem and error. Much of the damage school does can be done at home. Children can be methodically taught to hate learning. They can learn that reading is a difficult chore, that math is hard and frightening, and that history and science are boring. Many families starting off with a curriculum give up one way or another. Either the family moves to looser ideas about learning, or they send the children to school, or the children WANT to go to school instead of having the equivalent frustration at home.

Scientifically speaking, my children are not a control group. They're not isolated and kept purely away from school methods and messages. But what is unquestionable is that there are now thousands of children who are learning without formal teaching. They are learning from the world around them, from being with interesting and interested adults doing real work and real play. Instead of being put away with other children to prepare for life, they are joining life-in-progress right at birth, and never leaving "the real world."

Several factors were ripe for this to happen. Attachment parenting, spread in large part by La Leche League, became a part of the consciousness of hundreds of thousands of families. Breastfeeding children without a schedule, sleeping with children instead of leaving them to cry, and attending to children's needs instead of pushing them away has become more and more common every day. *The Continuum Concept*, a book and a philosophy by Jean Liedloff, based on her studies of more primitive cultures, reminded people that children learn best by observing adults living real lives. Maria Montessori had gone that direction, but still was isolating the children in schools with other children. John Holt died in 1985, but his magazine, *Growing Without Schooling*, continued for many years after that. Today we have resources that none of those named above had imagined when their various contributions unfolded: Children's books from Dorling Kindersley, Usborne, Eyewitness, and other non-fiction publishers of their ilk are far beyond the children's books of even twenty years ago. The photographs, text and resources in books designed for young children now surpass what was available to adults forty years ago, and they're available in used bookstores and libraries. Then there is the internet. Any family with a fairly new computer and an internet hookup has access to more information than most university libraries had 25 years ago, and more than some have now, barring their own internet access. We don't need to wait for a book to be published, nor even a magazine or newspaper. News unfolds before us, with photos, with video.

Many school supporters seem mentally to compare school to a 1940's farmhouse with only a Bible and an almanac; such places existed, and some might yet. For many, in the past, school was the only place with books and paper, and the only place where one could read Shakespeare or use a world map or a globe. Those conditions are gone, though. Shakespeare on video can be borrowed from a library, and the texts of the plays are online in searchable versions. Books and maps are no longer rare. A home can easily surpass a school now, for availability of current and historical information.

Accepting that resources are readily available, what else is different about unschoolers? How will unschooling change *your* world?

Teachers and specialists have theories about learning to read, and timelines for learning to read, and the crucial nature of this method or that method. They fear to wait. Unschoolers who have the courage to wait find that children learn to read as naturally as they learned to speak, walk or use a toilet. They learn to read as effectively and effortlessly as they learned to use eating utensils and cups. Some

learn it at four, and some learn at eight or twelve, but they can figure it out if they have input, opportunity, encouragement and peace.

My children learned to read without phonics lessons, without programmed readers, and without pressure. Kirby had two and a half lessons, and that cured me of doubt. I had taught reading, years before, and laying those two experiences side by side made me aware of the damage that whole mindset does. So I read to him, played word games with him, sang with him, watched movies with him, bought him video games and magazines to go with them, and from Nintendo gaming guides and magazines, he learned to read fluently when he was nine.

My other two read at ten and eleven. I was more relaxed, and though I was surprised that Holly read "late" (for a girl, I thought, unfairly), a year ago she wasn't reading and now she reads very well. It comes almost suddenly, once they "get it," and I'm convinced that it comes suddenly at school too, but teachers who want job security and paychecks disguise the process with years of exercises and read-alouds and worksheets until those loom large and the child is lost within. At some point a child either reads fluently or has given up trying.

Because my children learned to read without having been taught, they have no doubt whatsoever that they could learn anything else. Few things are as important or as complex as reading, yet they figured it out and enjoyed doing it. If I thought I had taught them, they too would think I taught them, and they would be waiting for me to teach them something else.

They have never been criticized for "not showing their work" when they do calculations in their heads. Mathematics, too, they have learned in fun ways for real reasons.

My children are different from most of their schooled friends. They are more like their fellow unschoolers. They are comfortable with people of many different ages, they are kindhearted, and tolerant. Because they haven't been shamed and molded by school life and expectations and "peer pressure," they're more willing to appear different without adding value to that appearance. Some schooled kids conform to become invisible, and some rebel to become visible, but my children are who they are, where they are, now. They're not embarrassed about their interests or hobbies, they're not afraid to wear used clothes, or to play with younger children, or to hang around with adults. Because they are respected, they are respectful.

Though messages from and about school have woven themselves into the fabric of modern society, there will now be those whose lives belie former "truths." When my children are adults, they will not sit quietly if they overhear "If you don't go to school, you'll never learn to read," or "If you don't go to school you can never go to college and get a job."

When they're grown they will vote, they will be examples, they will be advisors,

119

and they might be managers or politicians. They could become teachers, or educational researchers. The status quo will not look inevitable to them, but will be seen as conscious choice.

There are unschoolers in Canada, the U.K., the U.S., New Zealand and Australia, though some prefer the term "natural learning." Homeschooling is becoming legal in more countries all the time. There are groups and websites in many European countries, in Japan, and in India. Again, because of the internet, the isolation and fears of thirty years ago do not have to be relived by each family. There is an international foundation on which to build.

The world changes slowly, but it tends to stay changed. Flight was not possible before balloons. Food storage and transportation were difficult before canning and refrigeration. Without today's wealth of books, videos and online information, home learning would be much more difficult. We can live in the light of our shared knowledge and ideas, in freedom and with confidence, at the cutting edge of education's future.

This originally appeared on the website of
a magazine called *Children of the New Earth*,
and was written in July, 2003 at the editor's request.

Balancing in the Middle Ground

Should people live in the water in the middle of the ocean, or should they live on land as far as possible away from an ocean?

Quickly! What's your answer?

This was a trick question just designed to make you think. But people really do ask the same kinds of questions of themselves sometimes. In some people's heads, "Don't believe everything you read" turns into "Don't believe anything you read."

In the middle are things like "Believe things that make sense and seem to work after you've thought about them and tried them out," and "Don't believe something just because you read it, but wait for it to be confirmed by other more trusted sources, or by your own research or observance."

By thinking in extremes, "There is more than one truth" becomes "All things are equally truthful." Just because there are many truths doesn't mean there's no such thing as nonsense.

And so with children, neither leave them in the middle of the ocean, nor prevent all contact with water. Find the balance point that allows the two of you (and the rest of the family) to feel safe, connected, and healthy. Letting children do nothing is as extreme as letting them do everything. Doing everything for them is as wrong as doing nothing for them. Somewhere in the infinite range between everything and nothing will be a comfortable, productive range, and you will more easily find that familiar place as each new decision comes along.

New unschoolers can feel that they're moving between extremes, and it can take a while to settle where the whole family is content. Sometimes it takes years, but there are ways to feel better in the meantime.

If the old rules were that school is vital and "an education" (defined as the curriculum of an ideal school) is necessary, will the new rules be that school is not important and an education is not necessary? We don't make school disappear by turning the other way. It's still there. Our kids might want to go to school someday, in some form. We don't deny that knowledge is important by becoming unschoolers, but many come to prefer the idea of "learning" with its vast possibilities over the narrower "education."

My favorite "new rule" has always been that learning comes first. Given choices between doing one thing or another, I try to go toward the thing that's newest for my kids, and most intriguing. "New and different" outranks "We do it all the time, same place same way." But there *are* comfort-activities, and to be rid of all of them would be as limiting as to only do routine, same, safe things. So we find a balance. Or we tweak the same and the safe, changing it enough to make it especially memorable from time to time.

Lately a couple of people came to [online discussions] and said unschooling wasn't working for them. As has been reported by others before, they said they had stopped doing school, and then stopped making their kids do anything, and now their kids were "doing nothing."

Aside from the idea of the rich potential of their "nothing," the parents had gone from making their kids do everything, to "making them do nothing." And interestingly, it *did* make them "do nothing," at first. Or at least the parents couldn't see the new things they were doing.

Rather than moving from one edge of a dichotomy to the other, the goal is to move to a whole new previously unknown middle place. My model won't work in everyone's head (as we're not as plug-and-play as some would like to think), but here is one way to look at this problem: See if you have a dial in your mind that says "everything" at one extreme and "nothing" at the other. It's impossible for anyone to do everything or nothing. Maybe label it "too much" and "not enough" instead, and try for the midpoint. Replace any on/off switches in your mind with slide bars or dimmers.

Reconsider your energy source. If the parents aren't powering all decisions anymore, should the children take up the task of generating enough power to fuel their own learning? I wouldn't expect my kids to do that any more than I would stop feeding them and expect them to become hunter-gathers in the back yard if they wanted to survive.

Energy is shared, and that's how unschooling works. Whether I'm excited about something new, or my children are excited about something new, there's still newness and excitement enough to share.

Some parents label unschooling as "child-led learning," and so they think they're going from "parent led" life to "child led" life, but the balance point is that the family learns to live together harmoniously.

Harmony makes many things easier. When there is disharmony, everyone is affected. When there is harmony, everyone is affected too. So if it *is* six of one or half a dozen of the other (right between none and a full dozen), go with harmony instead.

And harmony expresses the same idea that balance does in these social instances. How you live in the moment affects how you live in the hour, and the day, and the lifetime.

Some have written that unschooling made their family life better. In every case I've seen, making a family's life better is exactly what makes unschooling work well. So which comes first? Neither grew wholly in the absence of the other.

There's a regular contributor to the message board named Lyle. He wrote, "Unschooling has had an incredibly positive impact on our lives, and not only in an educational aspect, but in everything we do. It's changed the way we live, the way we think, and the way we look at the world in general." Another day he wrote: "When I was about ten or eleven, I wanted to be a writer. (Still do, in fact.)"

Lyle writes well and frequently about his unschooling. He could choose to write nothing, or he could separate himself from his family to become a professional writer and write every day for many hours. Lyle writes, as do many other unschoolers, for real purposes. He shares what he has discovered and experienced for the benefit of others who want their families' lives to move toward unschooling. His writing is real, because it affects the thoughts and actions of others.

Lyle *is* a writer. Somewhere between writing nothing and being a wealthy professional author, many people write in the middle ground, and others' lives are changed.

We can come to see our children and ourselves as writers, poets, actors, musicians, engineers, philosophers, sculptors or scientists right where we are now, instead of as potential future poets or scientists.

Halfway between the past we can't change and the future we can only imagine, we find ourselves in the present. Not just the present year, but the present day; not just the present day, but the present moment.

Thank you for spending some of your moments reading this, and I hope you enjoy many present moments with your children!

Sandra Dodd has three children who haven't been to school. Kirby is 17, Marty is 14 and Holly turns twelve November 2. Keith Dodd, the dad, is an engineer for money. He's a woodworker, a musician and a medieval Viking for fun.

Home Education Magazine, November/December 2003

View from Shakespeare, in SW New Mexico

What Marty Really Needed

I have a teenaged boy now who can drive and who has a great computer he bought himself. It's a good combination for me, because while Kirby is driving himself the places I used to have to take him, I can stay home and play on his computer.

One Saturday night not long ago, I was playing on the computer in Kirby's room, and Marty came in. Marty was fourteen. By the time this is read, he might be older. But he was fourteen, it was Saturday, and I was playing something on Neopets.

Marty came in and said, "Mom, you know what I really need?" I didn't know. Had I been pressed to guess, I might've thought maybe he wanted the new Nickelback CD, or maybe a hamburger, or to win the lottery. Though his question had been more rhetorical, mine was real:

"What?"

"A map of the New Mexico Territory when Arizona was a part of it."

I might never have guessed that one, so I'm glad he told me. This was pretty exciting for me, because I figured I had such a map. So I led Marty right up to the library, which is full of my life's packrattish collection of books. He helped me move a pile of blankets and pillows and I pulled out my cache of New Mexico history books. One was *New Mexico in Maps* and three were school textbooks from years ago. There was a trivia book and a "roadside history," but the map book was the star of that show.

Feeling like an efficient librarian, I told him the textbooks were outdated and not to trust them, but the maps should still be good. I asked if he knew each had an index (to which he gave the impatient "YES, mom," because I was talking too much).

I went back to my game, feeling a little giddy that I had had what he asked for right in the house already.

After half an hour or so, Marty came back. He seemed kind of giddy himself. He told me that if Zachary Taylor hadn't died, New Mexico would've become a state sooner, and a bigger one, instead of waiting 'til 1912. And when he told that I had just a slight feeling that I'd heard it before, but it was nothing I "knew." Now Marty *knew* it, because he cared.

But alas for my library career, the maps I had weren't good enough. They didn't show that bit of southern Colorado. They were just modern maps with different markings.

Marty said, "I need to go to the state museum in Santa Fe."

"Palace of the Governors?"

"Yes. Hey, did you know the guy who wrote Ben Hur was governor of New Mexico?" (He had just read that, in one of my books.)

"Yeah. Did you know he wrote it in that building, while he was governor?" (He wrote some of it in Indiana, but finished it in Santa Fe.)

Here is why Marty wanted a map: He was designing a cowboy-themed role-playing game. He wanted to know which towns were around in territorial days, after the railroad came, and how people got between them. It was the same kind of research people do to write historical novels or movie screenplays.

I knew he wanted more than just a map. He wanted the best kind of history—factoid and trivia. So I reminded him of three human resources he has access to in his life. Pati Nagle is a friend of mine and former housemate who has written several novels about the Civil War in New Mexico. Jeff Cunico's grandfather and great grandfather were Italian coal miners in Trinidad, in southern Colorado, when it was part of the New Mexico territory. Jeff is a history buff, and he's Marty's godfather. The nextdoor neighbor at our old house, Mo Palmer, was photo archivist of Albuquerque for years before she went to teach history at a private school. A font of cool trivia and anecdotes, Mo has the interesting trait of knowing the history of buildings and sites. She grew up in Albuquerque and knows the history of every older building, and what was there before anything was built.

Life being what it was that month, I couldn't easily go to Santa Fe, so I convinced Marty to try the Albuquerque Museum first. There, in the Civil War section, was the map Marty needed. "I want this one." Sure he did! It was an original, published in 1857, in England. He said it was the perfect map for him, though.

In the gift shop there was a different territorial map, showing an engineering proposal for a railway. It's not where the railroads ended up being, though, so Marty didn't want it. They didn't have a copy of the English map.

I hoped to surprise Marty by finding a copy of that map he liked and buying it. No such luck, but I found it online with a "zoom" feature. We could look at it, but not own it.

With Google.com, I found a map dealer in Arizona and ordered two other maps for Marty that way. They cost less than $20 with shipping, and the dealer e-mailed saying he would refund me part of the shipping since those two were small. I wrote to thank him, and told him about Marty the homeschooled gamer saying he really needed that map. I got this in reply: "Oh-oh, If you're not careful, your son may have a future as an underpaid history teacher—or worse: a map dealer! Thanks for the background!"

A homeschooler wrote recently and asked how I fit learning opportunities into our lives. At first I had that feeling that I didn't understand the question, and then I thought of it another way. Can I describe how our lives are lived so that learning happens so effortlessly? I can try, and the first answer is simple. We just have fun.

Marty still wants to go the state museum in Santa Fe. Maybe we'll find a census or something that lists the towns in some snapshot way for Marty's gaming purposes. I've been informed of map archives at the engineering library at the university here, and so I have some transportation hours ahead of me!

The cool thing is that on the way to these places, Marty and I will get to talk about all kinds of things. Holly will probably go, and learn something cool, but I couldn't possibly predict what it will be. We'll have lunch in Santa Fe, and see the yellow aspens, and fresh snow on the mountains, and will probably make a memory or two that will last us for many years.

Nobody would encourage a child to spend hours at online role playing games with an "I need a map" result in mind, but that is one of many natural outcomes of my letting Marty do what he wants to do online.

"One thing leads to another." I've said it myself many times, but what I'm coming to believe is that with the addition of joy and encouragement, one thing leads to five or ten things, and each of them to five or ten other things, and so the whole world can open up from one map of territorial New Mexico, or from any other fun thing. Whatever is treated as an interesting portal to the universe can become one.

While you're living your life, open as many doors as you can.

Home Education Magazine, January/February 2004

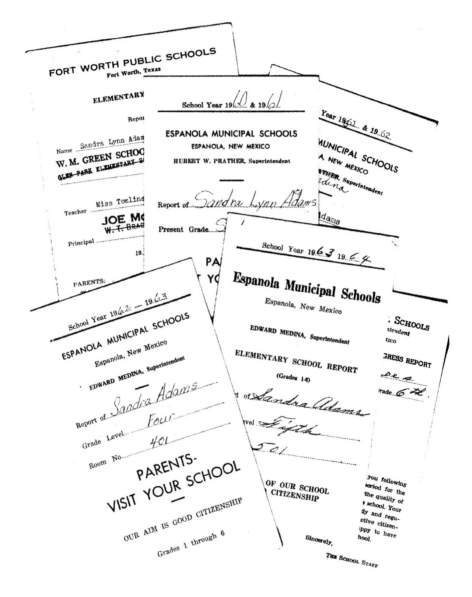

FORT WORTH PUBLIC SCHOOLS
Fort Worth, Texas

ELEMENTARY

Repo

Name Sandra Lynn Adam

W. M. GREEN SCHOO
GLEN PARK ELEMENTARY S

Teacher Miss Tomlin

JOE M
W. T. BRAE

Principal
19

PARENTS:

School Year 19__ & 19_61_

ESPANOLA MUNICIPAL SCHOOLS
ESPANOLA, NEW MEXICO

HUBERT W. PRATHER, Superintendent

Report of Sandra Lynn Adams

Present Grade S

Year 19_61_ & 19_62_

MUNICIPAL SCHOOLS
A, NEW MEXICO

THER, Superintendent
dina

dams

School Year 19_63_ 19_64_

Espanola Municipal Schools
Espanola, New Mexico

EDWARD MEDINA, Superintendent

ELEMENTARY SCHOOL REPORT
(Grades 1-8)

of Sandra Adams

vel Fifth

501

School Year 19_62_ — 19_63_

ESPANOLA MUNICIPAL SCHOOLS
Espanola, New Mexico

EDWARD MEDINA, Superintendent

Report of Sandra Adams

Grade Level Four

Room No. 401

PARENTS-
VISIT YOUR SCHOOL
—
OUR AIM IS GOOD CITIZENSHIP

Grades 1 through 6

OF OUR SCHOOL
CITIZENSHIP

Sincerely,

THE SCHOOL STAFF

. SCHOOLS
ntendent
cico

GRESS REPORT
DE A
rade 6 th

you following
eriod for the
the quality of
school. Your
ly and regu-
ctive citizen-
ppy to have
hool.

128

The School in my Head

"Nobody's perfect," they say, and I have been challenged to reveal my own doubts and failings. I don't mind.

I still have a school in my head. Witness my total unwillingness to go to Disney World. That is a definite "nope" for me, and the only thing that would help would be more deschooling. That might happen, but I would rather settle for the more comfortable Disneyland.

Here is the true and embarrassing reason that I can love Disneyland and fear Disney World: I can score a higher percentage at Disneyland. I can do better than 80%, maybe 90% if I stay three days. I have heard from many people that one would have to stay at Disney World a week to see it all. So I don't want to go, because if I see any less than 70% that would not be a passing grade.

I see the world in terms of percentage grades. I have a "grading" overlay behind my eyes somehow that still hasn't totally faded out. It's sad but true.

For some people it's even worse, though. Some people can't leave school because they're carrying it around like a snail and his shell. They live there, still. School became an ingrown, hard part of them. They still define themselves by their school failures and successes.

How does a person who has gone to school for twelve years or thirteen or sixteen or twenty years get over all that programming and all those messages? Slowly, and with effort, and sometimes school can still flood back in or ooze around the edges. Can they find their school-less selves?

Last year I forgot school was out, and offered to help a friend of mine in one of her history classes. It was July, though, and she said, "Cool! When school starts." She needed to borrow some chain mail, but not in summer. That seemed like progress, for me to have been unaware of "school year" for a while.

Every September, "back to school" kicks in. I crave the smell of crayons and new pencils. I like to go down the school supply aisle at the store and admire packages of paper, and new binders. My kids still have the binders they've had for years and they don't need new ones. I don't either, yet I'm drawn there like a migratory bird that has to pass over familiar ground at the same time every year.

I like the appearance of the letter "A" much better than I like to see a "D" or an "F." My maiden name started with "A" and my married name starts with "D." "D" is not as good. Those letters are branded into my brain with their "values" from school.

But little scars like that are only irritations or curiosities. I regret scars and imperfections and little sorrows, but though they slow me down, they don't cripple me. I can see through and over them.

School is part of me, and I am part of the school memories of many people, whether as a schoolmate or as their teacher. But school is not a part of my children, nor they of school.

Sometimes people say to me, "You're patient with your own children but pushy with unschooling parents." I don't go door to door asking people if they know about unschooling, and whether they'd like to know more. If they come where I already am, though, I might press. And when I do, it's because of the possibility that they will run out of time.

My kids have their whole lives to memorize 7x8 if they want to.

The mother of a twelve year old has VERY little time if she wants to help her child recover from school and spend a few unschooling years with him before he's grown and gone. She doesn't have time to ease into it gradually. If she stalls, he'll be fifteen or sixteen and it just won't happen.

If the mother of a five year old is trying to decide how much reading instruction and math drill to continue with before she switches to unschooling, I would rather press her to decide toward "none," because "some" is damaging to the child's potential to learn it joyfully and discover it on his own. And "lots" will only hurt that much more. "None" can still be turned to "some" if the parent can't get unschooling. But if she doesn't even try unschooling, she misses forever the opportunity to see that child learn to read gradually and naturally. It will be gone forever.
        Forever.

That's why I don't say, "Gosh, I'm sure whatever you're doing is fine, and if you want to unschool you can come to it gradually at your own pace. No hurry."

People say jokingly (though it's true) of their late-reading children, "I'm sure he'll be reading by the time he goes on a date." The same cannot be said of unschooling, though, if the parent is attached to thinking she needs to teach things.

Until a person stops doing the things that keep unschooling from working, unschooling cannot begin to work.

It seems simple to me. If you're trying to listen for a sound, you have to stop talking and be still.

Some people want to see unschooling while they're still teaching and putzing and assigning and requiring.

130

They have to stop that *first*. And then they have to be still. And then they have to look at their children with new eyes.

If they don't, it won't happen.

I still see "subject areas" everywhere, but I haven't taught those categories and prejudices to my children. Science has much more to do with history than geology has to do with microbiology, but in school geology, biology, astronomy and physics are all "the same thing," and history is different altogether. Yet the best parts of history involve the knowledge cultures had and how they put it to use, whether in shipbuilding or iron tool use, medicine or communications.

Holly asked yesterday about when people discovered the world wasn't flat. I told her there was no one date or century because people discovered different things at different times, and some were shushed up when they said the world was round, or that the sun didn't orbit around the earth. I also told her, "Ask your dad, because he's really interested in the history of science."

I noticed when I said it that I had "named subject areas," but I didn't feel too bad. She's twelve, and reading, and after all "the history of science" was never part of my schooling. A science teacher wasn't certified to teach me history, and vice versa. Only outside of school did I figure out that scientific discoveries *were* history, and that music was science, and that art was history.

School served to prevent connections for me, but I overcame that, with difficulty. It is a problem my children never had. If Animaniacs completed a circuit for them between Magellan and WWII, well it's a circuit school would never have completed for me under any circumstances. If learning for fun creates more connections than "serious learning" did, I can no longer look at "serious learning" seriously.

The best function of the school in my head, as it turns out, is to remind me where not to dwell. I did my time in and around school, and learned things painstakingly and grudgingly that my children later learned while laughing and playing and singing. I have guarded my children's freedom and given them happy choices that I didn't have.

I know from school that the best way to end an essay is to tie it back to the beginning, but these birds cannot nest where I started. They are a generation

131

removed and have flown freely out and about without a school to return to in September. But wait: if I take 10% off the essay for a weak ending, I do indeed tie it back, and so might yet get an "A."

Quite pathetic, but it makes me feel better.

Sandra Dodd lives in Albuquerque and has three tall young people in her family who have never been to school. A former teacher, former good student, Junior Honor Society member and one-time officer of the safety patrol, Sandra will probably never recover from school in this lifetime.

Home Education Magazine, March/April 2004

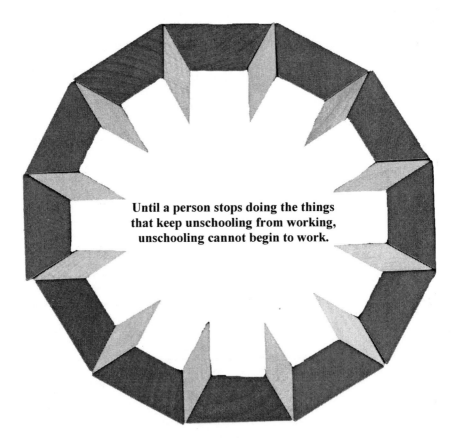

Until a person stops doing the things that keep unschooling from working, unschooling cannot begin to work.

Jubilation and Triangulation

Usually it looks like we're just playing around. When it doesn't look like we're playing, I work on it. Unschooling works best when we're playing around. Much of our play involves words, music and humor. It has to do with merrily connecting the dots, in a real world way, and in a mental-connection way.

Keith, my husband, loves *Babylon 5*, and the fourth season just came out on DVD.

At the end of one of the shows, the long-dark-haired Brit guy (I only know this show from passing through and staring for a bit and moving on, but someday I think I'll watch them all) is singing. And he's singing "Modern Major General" from *Pirates of Penzance*.

Our family knows Gilbert & Sullivan's *Pirates of Penzance* through the wonder of video, and because some people were cool enough to make a movie of it, which is great. Keith showed me that *Babylon 5* scene, in which the character sings all through the credits, and at the end of the credits someone says "CUT!" and he interrupts his singing to say "what"? Layers and levels of past and present and imagined future; fantasy and reality.

It was fun to think of a futuristic character singing something from the 1880s. It's like Data playing baroque music on *Star Trek TNG*, or when there was a Patsy Cline revival on the short-lived *Space: Above and Beyond* series. In all those cases, the science fiction connections came from my husband, and the musical documentation could come from me, and my kids had access to both.

I went back into the other part of the house where Holly was, and right out of the blue she said, "What is a hypotenuse?" I didn't know I had been singing this to myself: *"With many cheerful facts about the square of the hypotenuse."*

I stood and looked at her and thought two things: "Was I singing?" and "Do I know what a hypotenuse is?"

The answers were "I must have been," and "I think so."

I said, "I can't tell you, because you don't want to know the names of triangles."

She asked why I'd say that, and I said, "You told me you didn't want to know the names of triangles."

"And you believed me?"

"Yes."

While that was going on I had picked up a paperback dictionary that at hand and checked to make sure I was correct, because I have an abiding math-fright. But I had remembered correctly. When math can be in English—even English that came from Greek, which math terms often are anyway—I can usually remember it.

I said, "If a triangle has the corner of a square, has a right angle (and I showed her with my thumb and forefinger), then this long line (showed with my other hand) is the hypotenuse."

She looked at me for a long moment and said, "Oh! Okay." And she went back to playing Harvest Moon.

What it took to build up to that moment was Pirate of Penzance, Babylon 5, and some hours over a year or two of Holly and me playing a game called Math Arena.

Math Arena is a "buzz in when you know the answer" computer game. One of the contests is picking a match from an assortment of triangles, turned all kinds of directions, to the one they show. Holly can match or beat me at it, but when we first started I could beat her. Wanting to help her out, I had offered to tell her the names of the various shapes of triangles.

She said no, she didn't want to know their names; I should just let her do it her way.

I think in words. Keith likes a computer solitaire game done with mahjongg tiles. He likes to play it with national flags or Chinese symbols. I can only play it if I set the game to show letters of the alphabet. I can't play from just visual designs.

I play some other kinds of visual solitaire games but unless I can name the pictures, I can't play well. I can't hold an image in my head clearly enough to compare it against other things. Holly can. When the triangles come up on Math Arena, I have to think "isosceles" and then look for one (or "right" or "equilateral" or "obtuse" or whatever). Holly doesn't have to.

So my strewing plan was this: The next morning I would wake up early, make tea, and get out the geoboards. We have three. I would set up three basic triangles. When Holly got up and noticed these out, I would point at the hypotenuse on the right triangle. Either she would say "huh!" and "Would you make malt-o-meal?" and it would be over, or she might ask "And what are these other two?" Maybe it would be a couple of days of playing with triangles and maybe it will be one little "huh!"

That was my whole plan. I was going to be fine with however minor or glorious it was, because I knew she would have something to tie it to in her head, another dot to connect, and all that internal triangulation would be more valuable than any vocabulary study and formulaic recitation we could do.

But what happened was that I forgot to check back on my geo-board kid-trap. When I remembered in the early afternoon, Marty and Holly were working on fancy designs with colored rubber bands, and making "how many triangles?" puzzles for each other to count triangle within triangles. I came over and said, "That is a hypotenuse," and I pointed right at a green rubber hypotenuse. Holly said, "I know, I told him already." Not only had I missed my big chance to review it with her, she (at twelve) had already explained it to her brother (the fifteen year old).

We played a dictionary game one day that week with lots of people, about what languages various English words were originally from. One that was called out was "hypotenuse!" and I said without hesitation "Greek!" Holly was there, but neither of us said "Hey, they said 'hypotenuse'!"

The day after, we babysat some friends, and we were all playing Math Arena. The "game host's" name (which we had never had reason to note before) is "Felix Hypotenuse." "Felix" is from Latin, and is related to "felicity," another word they sing in *Pirates of Penzance*. It's fun for me that Holly enjoys that sort of trivia.

And so, after years of avoiding the term at Holly's direction, we had a week where "hypotenuse" came up repeatedly. It was fun, and it's a story worth telling, but it neither makes nor breaks any past or future learning. It's a small part of a big whole, one dot in countess millions. If Holly were to die soon, she wouldn't need to know any more about triangles than she knows today. If she lives a long life, she has all that time to learn more. She's playing, she's having fun, and she's learning.

Home Education Magazine, May/June 2004

Playing

Play can be serious business. Playing is certainly the main way that very young children learn, until they go to school.

What if they don't go to school? What if the ages of five and six don't mark a life change, and the playing progresses along naturally?

Many people would have no idea how to answer that question. The idea that toddlers' play would naturally progress to other levels without interruption, without separation from families, and without professionals telling children when, where and how to play is foreign to most in our culture.

In one small corner, though, it's common knowledge. There are unschoolers whose children have not been to school and who have continued to play.

Recently on a discussion list someone said sure, she understood how young children learn through play, but what about when they got older and stopped playing?

I have known people who stopped playing, but I was never one of them. In my last year of high school, my boyfriend who had already graduated built a kind of playhouse in the woods to be "our house." It was a hole under the roots of a cottonwood, dug out a little better, covered with branches and sticks found by the side of the Rio Grande behind the high school. I ditched school there a couple of times and met him. Was it dignified? No, it was like Neverland! In college I had another boyfriend and we had a running fantasy "plan" to live in the 1600s in England and run a really sweet, peaceful orphanage, filled with music. It wasn't long before I was involved in medieval doings with the Society for Creative Anachronism, which is an international medieval-themed life-size game.

As with all games, and all playing, there was reality too. We really made things and learned music and researched and made clothing and armor. We cooked real food. Then we put on our new clothes and our new names and played elaborate games.

My three children grew up around adults who played, not just putting on feasts and tournaments and building medieval-looking camps, but also playing strategy board games and mystery games, having costume parties when it wasn't even Halloween, and making up goofy song parodies on long car rides.

Maybe because I kept playing I had an advantage, but I don't think it is beyond more serious adults to regain their playfulness.

But (some might be thinking), if you just play all the time, how will you know the kids are learning? I knew my boys had learned all the swimming safety rules when they rhythmically took turns reciting them exactly wrong: Never swim with a buddy, always swim alone; Always swim in a storm; Always run by the pool...

There was no reason for me to say, "That's wrong." I would have spoiled their fun if I had. I didn't say a word. I knew enough already, because I had this information:
1) they knew all the rules
2) they understood the concept of opposites
3) they had a sense of humor and weren't afraid to use it.

"How do you know they're learning?" The people who ask that question are looking at the world through school-colored glasses. Those same parents knew when their children could use a spoon. They knew when the child could drink out of a cup. They knew when walking and talking and bike riding had been learned.

Here's how I learned that Kirby knew about the Huns: He was waiting for me to give him a ride, while I was talking on the phone to a local mom who was considering homeschooling. We were discussing unit studies, and I said they weren't necessary, that people just keep learning their whole lives. "You can't finish China," I said, and Kirby commented dryly, "The Huns tried that."

So, on my mental checklist, I note Kirby identifying the Huns, using the word in a sentence, knowing a dab about Chinese history. But was I testing? Was he reporting? Neither. He was just making a joke. And it was sufficient for me to discover what he knew.

All my life I was given advice like this:
Be serious
Act your age
Don't take this lightly.

Now, though, that I'm involved with unschooling I say to adults and to children alike, *take this lightly.* Play around.
Play with words, with ideas, with thoughts.
Play with music.
Play in the rain.
Play in the dark.
Play with your food.

But play safely. Play is only play when no one involved is objecting. It's only playing if *everyone* is playing.

The gentlest games can be dangerous. Tennis is a non-contact sport, but you could kill someone with a tennis racket. Chess is pretty passive, but humiliation can hurt permanently. Some adults I know (and, sadly, some children) avoid humor and avoid playing because they have been wounded by the alleged "just playing" of others.

The connection between humor and learning is well known. Unexpected juxtaposition is the basis of a lot of humor, and even more learning. It can be physical, musical, verbal, mathematical, but basically what it means is that unexpected combinations or outcomes can be funny. There are funny chemistry experiments, plays on words, math tricks, embarrassingly amusing stories from history, and there are parodies of famous pieces or styles of art and music.

Here are some recently-touched sources from our house:
    The Transitive Vampire
    The Marx Brothers
    Animaniacs
    Monty Python and the Holy Grail
    P.D.Q. Bach
    Weird Al
    The Reduced Shakespeare Company
    Eddie Izzard

From these and other books, videos, and sound tapes that are intended to induce hilarity, my kids (and my husband and I too) have learned about history, geography, grammar, literature, music, mythology and religion. There doesn't need to be any separation of learning and laughter.

While I was working on this article, I stopped to make waffles. An egg was cracked a bit in the carton and had dried back up over the hole. I could've put it quietly in the trash, but I took it to Holly and said dramatically, "This egg must be destroyed." She jumped right up to get it, and I told her I didn't know how long it had been broken, and she could throw it if she wanted to. She started out and I asked where she was going to do it. I could've made suggestions, but she had decided: "Off the deck!" That deck is a long way up there. Good choice.

She has broken eggs before. It wasn't new, but it's still fun. When she got back into the kitchen, she was excited to have missed her target. "I aimed for the dirt but I hit the beam (a railroad tie on the ground) and it broke and splattered."

If there are those among the readership who would prefer scholarly justification for living more creatively and lightly, you might read *Conceptual Blockbusting* by James Adams or *Free Play* by Stephen Nachmanovitch. Or you could skip the research, your children could be your teachers, and you might simply resolve to play more for their sake. The benefit to you will be a bonus.

Home Education Magazine, July/August 2004
Ressources Parents, Spring 2005 (translated to French)

Holly (and Mario on the computer)

The following article is offered as a sample exchange with an always-unschooled twelve year old. Encouraging and answering questions is one of the best tools unschooling parents can develop, and humor is another one. When I was young and was lucky enough to have anyone read to me, I was too often shushed if I interrupted to ask questions. If reading is for the sake of the child, and if learning is important, the interruptions are the most important parts!

Holly and the Bible

Holly has a fascination with religion. She doesn't believe it's true, yet she keeps coming back to religious questions.

This morning (fifteen minutes ago when I wrote this, two months ago when I put it online, January 2004 in the original) she was lying on the floor of my office looking up at shelves.

"What's *The Old Schoolhouse*?"

"A magazine about homeschooling by fundamentalist Christians."

"What's 'fundamentalist'?"

"They believe the Bible is literally true and that everything they need to know is in there and they live just by the Bible."

"Does the Bible say anything about keeping your kids home from school, or about sending them to school?"

"No, but it says things they interpret to be about school, so they quote that about homeschooling. Other people find verses to use to tell kids they need to go to school."

"Will you read me the whole Bible?"

"Sure. Now? I think I have one right in here." I did. I asked if I should start with the best parts or just start at the beginning.

She ignored that, and said "Are you going to trick me and read *Lord of the Rings*?"

"Don't you think you would know the difference?"

"I don't know."

So I started out with Genesis 1:1, and by 1:2, she said, "That's how *Lord of the Rings starts*! And there were dwarves and elves..." I said, "Well, the *movie*

141

does" and she laughed because she doesn't watch the movies either — she's very LotR resistant. But she did have a literary point, if she was thinking of the Galadriel voice-over at the beginning of *The Fellowship of the Ring*.

So I read on. She said "What's 'hethem'?" and she said it to sound quite a bit like "heathen." I explained that it was ". . .created *he them*," and did some rearrangement of words so she could get the grammar. I continued.

"So God spoke English?"

"No, he probably spoke Hebrew."

"Then shouldn't they have used the Hebrew words for 'day' and 'night'?"

I knew I'd never get past the first page. She was already frustrated that God has been misquoted. The King-James-worshiping fundamentalists would not have understood her objections.

After "moveth" and "creepeth," Holly said, "HEY, that's like that game!" And by that, she meant the then-new Strongbad parody of Zorg, which sayseth everythingeth in very-bad parody of 17th centuryest Englisheth ("Thy Dungeonman" at homestarrunner.com).

After one repetitive passage she said, "Hey, this is like poetry, but it doesn't rhyme."

"Maybe it did in Hebrew."

"Well poetry that doesn't rhyme is the worst kind."

And once she said "You wrote this!" and she pointed to the cover of the Bible, which sure enough had my name in gold, right on the front, so I told her, "Yeah, I guess I did."

When I got to "dominion" over things she asked what that meant. I said it meant we owned them, that we were kings over animals and could tell them what to do (thinking "yeah, like things that creepeth are going to listen").

Holly says, "And yet we're not king of the forest!?"

So at the end of the sixth day, that was the end of the first chapter and I said so. She said, "That was a short chapter. Wait, I thought it was divided into books."

"Yeah, Genesis is a book, and it has fifty chapters. When you want to tell someone something particular, you tell them which book, chapter and verse," and I showed her.

That was enough Bible for her for today.

She might or might not come back for more, but she made more intelligent comments and asked more questions that actually meant something than some people would be willing to ask in a year of Sunday School. And she made connections with *Lord of the Rings*, homeschooling, language, journalistic integrity, Strongbad, poetry and *The Wizard of Oz*.

So it goes.

Sandra

P.S. "So it goes" reminds me of Kurt Vonnegut's *Slaughterhouse Five*, and of Linda Ellerbee who ended her TV news commentaries with that line. And so it goes, connecting the dots.

Acorns, March 2004, as "A Fascination with Religion"

Kirby dressed for the Los Alamos prom, 2003

No Graduation for Kirby

When my son Kirby was six and seven years old and I talked about unschooling, I was confident but much was theoretical. When he was nine I was asked to speak at conferences. Some people rolled their eyes in those days and said, "Yes, well... her oldest is little. She doesn't know what she's talking about."

As I write this, my children are 17, 15 and 12. Now when I'm pooh-poohed, it's by people saying, "You couldn't really understand the problems of a mother with several very young children in the house, since all of yours are older."

You do the math.

I entered the world of unschooling with a five year old. I'm about to peek out the other end, as Kirby turns 18 this summer.

Were we using a curriculum, Kirby would "graduate" by finishing the senior-level coursework. And it might have been last year, or next year. There are 18 yr olds still in high schools, all over the country. But let's say he had done that, and finished "on schedule." He would have the equivalent of a public high school education now, and be done.

How is a life of natural learning "done" though? When is "graduation" for an unschooler?

A few years ago, I used to think a big 18th birthday party, maybe all weekend at a lodge in the mountains, could serve as a rite of passage. The more my husband and I discussed the purposes and reasons, the less clever the plan seemed. We didn't want to draw a line between his childhood and "being grown," with its implications of "we've finished our job," or "time to move out!"

So just as I can calmly say "We don't do grades, but Holly is twelve," I will just start saying "He's eighteen," not "He graduated from homeschooling."

WHAT ABOUT COLLEGE?

I remember college well. Most undergrads I knew were there against their will to some extent, or with no purpose other than to get away from home. Some had chosen to go 2000 miles from their families out of a combination of spite and avoidance. If they had to go to college, they were going to make sure it was expensive and inconvenient for their parents. Many had majors they didn't want, were forbidden to dabble, and were punished if their report cards were bad. The loss of emotional or financial support loomed over them for infractions of their parent's plans for their lives. Some of them were twenty-one years old, give or take a couple of years, and their parents were still telling them what classes to take.

It baffled me. I wanted to be in college. I had gone early, and finished in four years. I was 20. But looking back, the glorious thing about college for me was the music, the art, the freedom of movement among people who were from places other than my hometown, who knew things I didn't know, and who would stay up late and talk about life, and the world, and how people are. My kids have had those things all their lives.

My husband, Keith, finished college at 29 after years of changing majors, having a rich and interesting life, holding jobs that paid little but from which he learned a lot and met interesting people. That was quite a while ago—a lifetime, in Kirby-terms. For years now he has been an engineer, respected by colleagues, and secure in his career. They don't care that it took him nearly twelve years to finish college.

Most readers here could probably name friends who have expensive degrees they don't use, and other successful, happy friends without college credit, or college expenses.

So back to this never-schooled seventeen year old at our house.

Will he go to college? Maybe.
In September this year? No.
Are we worried? No.

Maybe we're surprised not to be worried.

Maybe he wants to be a programmer, or a lawyer, he has said. He's not in a hurry. He might like to take some classes in the winter at TVI (a technical school near our house that offers basic classes transferable to the university in town).

The calm surrounding all this surprises me, but it shouldn't. We weren't too worried when he read "late" (meaning later than we thought he might; he was nearly nine). We didn't withhold our regard as he made various choices in his life, and he has impressed us and others many times with his competence and demeanor. Adults trust him. Kids like him. Not all people his age have even that, but Kirby also has a job he has had for four years. That's longer than some adults have held a job. He works at a gaming shop, and so he is surrounded by bright, interested and interesting people. He is active at the karate dojo he attends. He teaches a beginning class once a week. Some his age will take karate for the first time in college, if their parents let them study anything so frivolous.

I would rather Kirby never go to college than to go without a reason to go. I would rather he continue to learn from experiences around him, from reading, the internet, friends, movies and direct observation than to borrow a bunch of money (or spend ours) to attend college just because his grandparents or uncles or my neighbors might be impressed. If he did that, I would start to think maybe he wasn't as bright as we liked to think.

146

If and when he has a desire or need to go, we will support him fully. If he enrolls, it will be because he has a reason to go, and has made a free choice. Those factors will create an entirely different experience from some of those around him who were pressured to go and are now angry with their parents and the world. And he doesn't have the motivation to get as far from home as he can. He *likes* home.

Why am I surprised? It is just more of the continuum of life off the assembly line.

Live Free Learn Free #1, August/September 2004

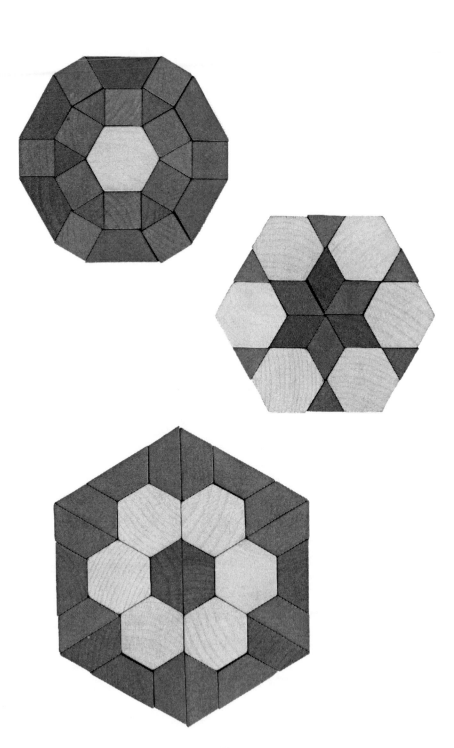

Three Readers

Two and a half reading lessons—that's all Kirby ever had. And then he learned to read? No, then I learned not to teach reading. Maybe I should've learned that lesson in school, though, when I "taught reading" the first year I was hired. I wasn't a reading specialist, but they didn't have one, so they gave me the 125 lowest scoring 7th graders and called it "reading." At 12 and 13, most of them read some, and a few read not at all, though they'd been in school for six or seven years before that.

It would be different, I thought, with homeschooling. One on one, no competitive pressure, no grades. And unschooling? Reading to him and playing with him would be all it took.

I was right, about that last part but what I hadn't learned yet, in 1992, was that each person's development is his very, very own and even in the absence of competitive pressure and school's schedules, there are people who aren't nearly ready to read at the age of six or seven.

Kirby learned to read privately, in some way unknown to me, and gradually. The book he first read fully and fluently and as well as any adult could was *NES Game Atlas: The Nintendo Player's Guide*, as he was working through the original Mario game. From that same book he had already learned map reading and deductive reasoning (solving the bonus round from the chart showing the only eight permutations the matching game had).

By the time Kirby was reading well and my worries were calmed, Marty was five and had decided to stay home too. We had thought maybe he would opt for school, but he chose home.

Marty had the indicators pointing to dyslexia: left handedness, skill at puzzles requiring spatial reasoning and sequencing, and confusion between similar-looking letters and numbers. My dad was that way. Marty's dad was that way too, so I didn't expect Marty to read early. We kept him supplied with Lego, mazes, and puzzles of all sorts. He saved his allowance and bought a used Playstation, and a game called *Breath of Fire III*. I found a used player's guide for it, removed the binding, put each page in a sheet protector, and he decorated a three ring binder for it. That was Marty's reading primer, and he learned to read as well as anyone, without lessons. He was nine. The vocabulary in that book was not simple or childish. It was aimed at teens and adults.

Holly's a girl, and girls are verbal, and girls read earlier, I thought. By eight, when Kirby had been reading, Holly wasn't even nearly so. By nine, when Marty had read, nothing. I wasn't as worried as I would've been had she been my first, and that was good for her. At ten, though, Holly started to worry because other homeschoolers she knew were reading and she wasn't. Younger kids were reading. One family was using her as a bad example: *"You need to do these lessons so you won't turn out like Holly, who can't even read."*

A couple of incidents greatly expanded what I had known before, though, and have changed my entire view of late readers. Holly was in a summer dance and theatre "camp," a five-full-day set of sessions. I told the teachers she wasn't a reader and requested they not ask her to read aloud. They were using the book *Barn Dance* for the production, so we bought a copy a couple of days before, and I read it to her several times. By the performance, some kids hadn't memorized their assigned verse, but Holly had memorized hers and everyone else's too. The same thing happened when she was in a play. She couldn't be dependent on a script she couldn't read, and ended up memorizing the whole thing over the course of the rehearsals.

Later that year, she joined girl scouts, and I told the leaders she wasn't reading. A schooled friend of hers offered to help her, but the "help" consisted mostly of reminding the other girls and Holly that she, the friend, had to help Holly read. Because that was the first time in their lives the friend had been a step ahead of her, Holly let it slide. There was a presentation for parents one night. While the other kids were reading off paper, mispronouncing "Juliet Lowe," mumbling and covering their faces, Holly's portion of the program was clear, involved eye contact and her own words

When she was eleven, I wrote this:
> Holly wasn't reading at ten. She wasn't happy about it, either. She is at the point now where she is reading words without meaning to. For fun she tries to walk around the house without recognizing any words. At eleven, she's still not reading chapter books. But if you met her and talked to her you wouldn't think for a second, "I bet this kid doesn't even read," because there's not much she can't talk about, and if she knows nothing about it but it sounds interesting, she'll ask intelligent questions."

Though Holly wasn't reading, her vocabulary was sophisticated and she was fascinated by the history of and connectedness of words. When she did start to read, she had no reason to use easy books. She was still eleven when she did her first real reading, a Judy Blume novel. She read two of those, and moved on to Steven King's novella *The Body.*

When she had only been reading a couple of months, we were sitting down to watch "TheTwilight Zone," Holly reached over to move the Tank Girl comic books she had been reading. One was called "The Odyssey." Then the DVD menu came up, and one of the episodes was "The Odyssey of Flight 33." She commented on it, and I said "You saw the word 'odyssey' twice in an hour? Cool!"

She said, "I saw the word 'odyssey' twice in one *minute!*"

Kirby reads like a lawyer. He can skim a rules book or instructions for a game, and explain simply and clearly to others. If he forgets a detail, he'll be able to find it easily. Marty likes humor and history. Holly's main reading is on the internet, but she likes name books, and other non-fiction and trivia. One thing she doesn't use the internet for is definitions and spellings. She likes my old full-size *American Heritage Dictionary*, and will sprint upstairs to look something up on the slightest excuse. Meanwhile, I've come to rely on Google as my dictionary, thesaurus and spelling guide.

As their reading ability unfolded and grew, I learned things I never knew as a teacher, and that I wouldn't have learned as an unschooling mom had they happened to have read "early." Reading isn't a prerequisite for learning. Maps can be read without knowing many words. Movies, music, museums and TV can fill a person with visions, knowledge, experiences and connections regardless of whether the person reads. Animals respond to people the same way whether the person can read or not. People can draw and paint whether they can read or not. Non-readers can recite poetry, act in plays, learn lyrics, rhyme, play with words, and talk about any topic in the world at length.

I have three teenagers now, all of whom read very well. Their learning was not slowed down or put on hold for premature or frustrating "reading lessons," except for those two and a half short lessons Kirby suffered, which I would take back if I could.

Reading will happen, and if it takes longer for your children than you think it will, keep them happy and distracted in the meantime. As their experience and vocabulary grow, their reading will be that much more effortless the day they're fully equipped to understand the written word.

Live Free Learn Free #5,
May/June 2005

151

Sandra and Kirby, summer 1998

(This photo didn't make the original interview space-cuts.)
Photo by Kirby's Aunt Irene

This was edited to meet the length limitation when it was first published, and with Emily's permission, here is the original version:

An Interview with Sandra Dodd

Finding clear ideas and a philosophy of learning is a daunting task. We may strain to hear a voice that solidifies our ideas concisely and fortunately for many unschoolers, Sandra Dodd's vocal presence is a bright spot of lucidity. Her mind is a virtual box of magic, her innovative ideas for learning are just plain fun, and her passionate belief in unschooling articulates a philosophy of life.

A former junior high school teacher, Sandra lives with her family in New Mexico. Her three children have never been to school. She serves as editor of the HEM Online Newsletter, and is host of the weekly HEM Unschooling chat. Sandra travels the country spreading the word about unschooling whenever she can and is currently writing her first book.[4]

With clarity, certainty and humor, Sandra's wisdom reminds us to keep asking questions and maintain flexibility when looking at the world. Recently, I was able to attend Sandra's workshops at a homeschooling conference and as a new unschooler, I was struck with the depth of her conviction. Our subsequent e-mail correspondence led to the following interview.

Unschooling may appear overwhelming to some people who misunderstand its fundamentals. Why do you think it's difficult to understand the concept of unschooling and why are many folks aggressive in their attacks of its philosophy?

People attack what they don't understand. I think I stole that line from a movie. There's a lot to be learned in movies. I could take a class on philosophy, but I've picked up so much "ground fall" philosophy that it's starting to fit together like a 1500 piece jigsaw puzzle, and I never had to "study" or concentrate or take a test. The real test is whether people can apply what they've learned to everyday situations.

Those who went to school (and that's over 99% of those reading this) have based half their lives, give or take a decade, on school's rhythm and labels and categorizations. When things like "the school year" are as much a part of a culture as "family" and "sunrise," it's a radical departure to consider that maybe one of those three is unnatural. For many people, it disturbs the fabric of their lives. Some people's life-fabric is already kind of rumply, or they hated school and are *glad* to consider alternatives, but for those orderly folks

---

[4] And seven years later, finishing it, notes the editor, seven years later.

who have life all neatly arranged in their heads, who do more accepting than questioning, unschooling is a disturbing thing. They literally cannot understand it. It's too foreign to what they have always accepted as natural and inevitable.

You taught public school. What led you to unschooling?

When I taught I didn't go by the book. I didn't use the textbook. We used games and things I made up (handout-type things, I mean, and projects) and sometimes things the kids made up. I could go on and on about this, but it's off the topic so I shall restrain myself (I hope). We played with dictionaries a great deal. Every Friday we "just" did a ballad. Every Friday I sang them a ballad and provided the words. Afterwards I'd talk about what was interesting about the story, what else it seemed related to in folklore or other songs, how old it was believed to be, and what the evidence was. I didn't do it in a teacherly way, and for most of each school year many of the kids thought we were "doing nothing" on Fridays, that it was time out. No homeschoolers will be surprised to hear that the kids learned more on Fridays than any other time of the week, but because it was low pressure and there was no "accountability" it was joyous and easy.

Every single year some kids would moan when they got a glimpse of the first 20-verse ballad, "Aww, do we have to *memorize* this?" I'd assure them they did *not* have to learn it, but by the end of the year through requests for repeats of their favorites, I doubt there was a kid there who couldn't have sung at least one of the ballads and maybe ten from memory.

That was a heck of a lab to have, and most unschoolers don't have that advantage when they start out, of having seen "loose" learning situations up close. I was brave enough to try them when I was teaching because in college I'd been assigned to read lots of school reformers, including John Holt. This was in the early 1970's, at the height of the open classroom movement, and my professors believed in that principle so strongly and calmly that it just sounded like simple truth to me.

What happened was that it couldn't work in practice when kids were compelled to be in school. It works best when kids have the option to come or go, but in some very real ways the purpose of school is to keep the kids in the building, which defeats the benefits of natural learning. That's why I think so many schools gave up on it—that and they couldn't imagine it would work, and if you can't imagine it you can't do it.

What proof do you have that it is working? How would you suggest parents reassure themselves that this path is providing everything their children need?

Well starting at the end, there is *no* path that will provide everything for a child. There are some that don't even *begin* to intend to provide everything their children need. Maybe first parents should consider what it is they think their children really need.

As to proof of whether unschooling is working, if the question is whether kids are learning, parents can tell when they're learning because they're there with them. How did you know when your child could ride a bike? You were able to let go, quit running, and watch him ride away. You know they can tell time when they tell you what time it is. You know they're learning to read when you spell something out to your husband and the kid speaks the secret word right in front of the younger siblings. In real-life practical ways children begin to use what they're learning, and as they're not off at school, the parents see the evidence of their learning constantly.

But there is no evaluative evidence available and doubts of success can be a significant source of questioning the unschooling philosophy.

What would evaluative evidence look like? First, I'm not sure there is none available, but I'm sure I don't need any myself. If I had a financial dependence on other people accepting unschooling (that is, if I were selling it), then I would want some data to back up my claims. I'm living it, though, and it's not scaring me, and so I'm not looking for statistics to prove that I'm justified in seeing what I'm seeing. Do the schools have evaluative evidence? They have some evidence, but is it a clean catch? Where's their control group? Either what I was taught in school (three or four times) about scientific method is wrong, or the schools are based on faulty results, as their "test" was not set up according to the method they themselves espouse. How do they really know that every kid in their school didn't learn math and reading at home during the 185 days they're *not* in school? Or during the many-more-than-six hours they're home on those 180 school days?

I'm going to be part of their control group for the future. They need to know whether some kids can learn those things without being subjected to all the measures and instruction school is based on.

Actually there are researchers who have proven years ago that the principles of interest-based learning work best, but because it can't work well in a school atmosphere, it goes by the wayside, pretty much. Homeschoolers, though, can pick it up and run with it.

One of the many things that give me confidence is that I've looked teenaged unschoolers right in the eyes and talked to them, and seen thoughtful, whole and confident people. I've looked hundreds, maybe over a thousand, schooled kids in the eyes and seen fear, defiance, shame and other such defensive things. Maybe it was because I was a teacher or the parent/guardian of a friend of theirs, but the ability of schooled kids to interact with adults is purposely discouraged. Kids in school are expected to defer to adults and obey them and fear them, not much more. So they avoid them during their "off hours," and during the school day they just avoid eye contact.

What long-term benefits do you believe unschooling holds for your children?

If I saw it simply as a means to get them to college, I might be nervous. I see it as a way to live. I don't see it as keeping the kids out of college or hampering their opportunities for formal learning if they go that route, I'm not holding college up to them or me as "the goal." The goal, for me, is that they will be thoughtful, compassionate, curious, kind and joyful. That's all. That's not asking much, is it? I think if those traits are intact in them, they will continue to learn their whole lives.

A quote from you: "I don't really know the magic words to get people to be calm and realistic about expectations and results. To proceed without looking into the school-windows-of-their-minds all the time." If this is so, how can regular folks convince themselves that unschooling will work?

There is no switch I can flip. Just with other teaching/learning situations, all the learning takes place inside the learner. None can be inserted by a teacher.

If budding unschoolers will look at how they learned things *outside* the classroom, and use that as a model and a goal, that helps. They don't really have to hunt down other unschooling families, although it doesn't hurt. A family isolated from other unschoolers might do well to brainstorm examples of things they've learned informally and naturally, and to look around for other people learning things in the same manner.

Take unschooling itself or homeschooling in general. Who went to college to learn *that*? Whoever might read this later, are they doing it "for credit"? Are they doing it as an assignment they're required to complete? (Well, maybe there are a few husbands who will be "persuaded" to read home-schooling articles somewhat against their will...) No, I think they're learning about unschooling because they have a need and a desire to know.

You believe that unschooling cannot be a part-time affair. Given that, is it possible to unschool one child while another is using a structured curriculum? What if one child wants to go to school?

I believe that ideal learning takes place when everything is considered valuable, and the parents don't single out one or two subjects to "teach." I think that spoils the integrity of the set-of-everything, to say, "Math we won't risk, but the rest of that you can learn on your own, or not." It sets up an object and a field. Math is a Must-Know, and the rest is less valuable. I think setting "academics" apart from the rest of cool stuff to know is just as bad. Is science more important than auto-mechanics? HEY, it IS auto-mechanics, everywhere but at school, where auto-mechanics is in one building, and has one teacher with one set of credentials, and science is in another building, different teacher, different book, different line on the report card. In real life there is no single building, teacher, book, line or report card. There are thousands of buildings, and teachers, and books.

If one child in a family is using a curriculum because he or she wants to, and the work is done her own way, that's not as disruptive as I think it would be if the parent were inflicting a curriculum on one child while claiming or attempting to leave another child free to learn naturally. How could one prevent comparing? Maybe if the personalities were sufficiently different and the parents had no doubts that unschooling would work it would be doable. I wouldn't recommend it, though.

What I have recommended and can't get out of is that if one of my children wanted to go to school, I would go along with it. I have several justifications behind this. One is that I think the worst thing about school is the powerlessness of the students. They *have* to be there whether they want to or not, so there's no virtue in those who want to be there, and no joy in those who do NOT want to be. When families force their children home but the children would rather have stayed in school, the same powerlessness exists. I want my children to be home because they want to be. I try not to turn my kids against school. Every year I've asked each if they're happy with the way things are, and whether they might like to try school. We talk about it a bit, and they've always said, "I want to stay home." So far so good; if they change their minds I would be scared and nervous and irritated with the idea of having to get on a schedule and live around the school year, but I'd try go with it. Part of the reason I would go with it is that I would not expect it to last. I've made their home-life pretty fun, and school would have to be fantasyland to compete with what they have at home.

In any case in which a child is in school and the parents want to divorce themselves from the school instead of being fully involved and supportive, they might just shift a few degrees to where they let the kids (and teachers if necessary) know that homeschooling IS an option, and that if the child wants to stay in school he's responsible for his self-chosen involvement, not the parent. If the parent has separated learning from school in his or her mind, the pressure on a school-kid will be *much* lower than if the parent really believes this is the source of knowledge and success. Unschooling parents will be confident that the child can and will learn in spite of school, and around school, and maybe even in school, but they won't depend on the school to "educate" their child fully and completely as so many parents seem to do.

So while I think it's luxuriously easy if everyone in a family is committed to unschooling, I don't think life will be over for them if some of them are involved in formal learning. I think where unschooling and formality are side by side, unschooling will win out every time, because it's joyous and friendly.

You once wrote: "We have voices and ghosts inside us, and conditioning, all of which keep us from homeschooling clearly and joyfully and calmly. We have guilt and fear and "ideas" [BAD ideas] tied up with our thoughts of learning/education, and it just gums up our brains and our hearts." Tell us more about what these "bad ideas" might be, and about the importance of "deschooling."

People think learning has to happen on a schedule, and incrementally, and they get that idea from "courses" of study, and school years and semesters and graded textbooks. People fear that if teachers go to school for years to become teachers that they must KNOW something and that this arcane knowledge is the key to learning. People fear that without "A Permanent

Record" their child will grow up without an identity, without a reality, and might never get married or reproduce. School phrases like "being a student is a full-time job" and "what you do here will affect your entire life" and "you have to learn to get along with people, [so no, we're *not* going to transfer you to a teacher you can stand]", live in the heads of people who went to school for twelve to eighteen years, and if we didn't question them then, are we safe to question them now, with our tender children's futures in the balance? Those kinds of fears.

Another level of questioning comes along: "If this was *not* necessary, how might my own life have been different if I had not been subjected to school and all its shame and labeling and pressure?" For me these questions were much addressed by four years in Adult Children of Alcoholics, which meetings I attended from before I was pregnant with my first until after the birth of my second. I've accomplished a lot of personal healing and family progress by treating my children the way I wish I could have been treated when I was their age. Instead of using a script from my own childhood, instead of saying what my mom or one of my teachers would have said to me, I really look at my own child and I try to say what they need to hear, what will make their life and learning easier and less stressful.

Deschooling means dismantling the overlay of school. Gradually (or just all of a sudden, if you have that ability) stop speaking and thinking in terms of grades, semesters, school-days, education, scores, tests, introductions, reviews, and performance, and replace those artificial strictures and measures with ideas like morning, hungry, happy, new, learning, interesting, playing, exploring and living.

I've been a teacher. From that point of view the world IS most definitely revolving around years and semesters, school districts, standardized test schedules, federal title monies, school bus contracts, cafeteria funding, library cuts, parking-lot pavement... all kinds of stuff that has nothing much to do with kids, their hearts, spirits and ideas. Shuck it away. Don't live there.

You believe that everything is educational. Is that for you the essence of unschooling, the bottom-line?

Yes.

You are clearly unwaveringly committed to unschooling. Why are your convictions so concrete? What makes you completely sure of this choice?

For whatever reason, I have very clear memories of childhood, and more than what happened (which I remember pretty well, some incidents back to baby days), I remember what I was thinking and feeling. I remember as early as second grade, talking to the other kids about their feelings and theories. I decided when I was in first grade that I wanted to be a teacher, so in parallel with the kid-interviewing (not really, but I did find a lot of talkative friends) I

159

was watching the teachers because I wanted to steal the good ideas for when I grew up. If I'd known I would grow up to be an unschooler, I couldn't have had better preparation.

Many teachers and parents have forgotten what it felt like to be little, and what sorts of things they could and could not understand in those days, so they end up expecting too much or too little of kids. They tend to present information as though it exists as a block that can't be broken down, instead of letting the child take in bits of it now and then according to his needs and his ability to understand. People don't take in pre-measured blocks of information. They assimilate one new thing at a time. Giving someone 25 pieces of information in five minutes is only useful if the recipient is very actively engaged in the situation. If they're not alert and curious, giving *one* piece of information is a waste of time. So for that reason I think it's better to provide clues and let others pick them up, rather than making an appointment with a person for the purpose of attempting clue-insertion. That's not how learning works best.

I went off on a tangent, but often the best stuff is off on tangents, not on the prescribed trail. That's true in conversations, on vacations, and in learning. If you're telling your kids all you know about Egypt and they ask how big baby crocodiles are, are you going to say, "Wait, I'm not through telling you about the three best theories on the construction of pyramids" and keep going with your lecture? The kid's the one doing the learning. Maybe in a year he's going to say "How did they make those pyramids without cranes?" and *then* you unfold all the rolling/floating/levitation theories you've ever heard in your life. (Levitation is a bit of levity—I was thinking of Kurt Vonnegut's "variable gravity" principle in which he suggested that gravity goes through phases like the weather does, and just as there are ice ages, there are periods of heavy and light gravity, and on a light gravity day the stones were just chucked up there).

I'm completely sure of unschooling because I believe in people's desire and ability to learn wonderful things in quirky ways if they're given the opportunity. Some people don't believe in unschooling, and one reason, I think, is this: They have a mental vision of "high school graduation"—of a set of facts and skills. They see that as their goal and destination. They work backwards from that incrementally and they want to put their kids on the straight and narrow road to that goal. They look at unschoolers, and they don't think unschoolers can get to their goal, so they reject any further thought of it. I think it's their goal that's straight and narrow.

If I wanted my children to reach high school graduation, I'd put them in school. That model channels all of life toward one small set of information on one small day (May 22 of the year the child is closest to his 18th birthday), after which the project ends. The model I'm operating on channels all of life toward a greater appreciation and understanding of all of life and it never ends, barring incapacitating brain damage or death. School and school-at-home sometimes teach people not to learn, or at least not to learn anything for fun without direction because "it won't count." I think everything counts. I think everything can be fun. When I say "I think," I very often mean "I am absolutely convinced after years of careful consideration and observation with no evidence to the contrary, and my original idea became a theory which has become a conviction."

Most of the best stuff I learned as a kid I learned in girl scouts, 4-H, from involvement in music of one sort and another, from visiting friends' homes and asking questions about the stuff there—houses are like museums, when they're not like hotel rooms. I really don't like hotel-room houses, but real houses are museums. I think a house that's like a hotel room might be hard place in which to unschool. I remember the geography and anthropology (I didn't know that term but I was collecting the facts and ideas in advance) I learned came from a Rocky & Bullwinkle quiz game I ordered off a cereal box. It had punch cards to mount on a little frame, and if you put the pointer into the right hole a light bulb came on. That's what programmers were doing in the early 1960's to make my life better. I loved that toy, and learned what I would have learned in a year in school. I got a series of National Geographic booklets with a sheet of perforated photo-stickers printed in color I had to lick and stick on the right pages. Sometimes the taste of certain stickers reminds me of pictures of Thailand even today! The teachers at school thought they had taught me all that geography. I'm sure they were proud.

So with my kids, I got them a GeoSafari[5], some geography games for the computer, and they get the mystery adventures from Highlights, and none of that is considered learning, just playing around. They play with maps, draw them, follow them, ask me a hundred questions, but I don't think they know the scope and definition of "geography." Someday they'll figure it out, and by the time they do they'll know so much about so many people and places it won't occur to them that they should have waited until they were older, or that it even needs to be named and categorized, since it's so integral a part of the fabric of Everything, and they're learning about Everything.

Since unschooling is a lifestyle, how can a family wanting to embrace these ideals begin the process? What encouragement would you offer?

Play. Joke. Sing. Instead of turning inward and looking for the answer within the family, within the self, turn it all inside out. Get out of the house. Go somewhere you've never been, even a city park you're unfamiliar with, or a construction site, or a different grocery store. Try just being calm and happy together. For some families, that's simple. For others it's a frightening thought.

---

[5] GeoSafari is an outmoded antique kind of electronic quiz game that was cool in those days, but I wouldn't recommend it in the days of high speed internet.

Try not to learn. Don't try to learn. Those two aren't the same thing but they're close enough for beginners. If you see something *educational* don't say a word. Practice letting exciting opportunities go by, or at least letting the kids get the first word about something interesting you're all seeing. If a family experimenting with unschooling can try to go some amount of time—a week, a month—without learning anything, but during that time they keep active, talkative, busy with life, maybe some art, some music, theatre or movies, walks to collect things (in the woods, in the dumpsters, it doesn't matter)—just *being*, but being busy—at the end of that time (or halfway through) I think it will become apparent that learning cannot be turned off. Given a rich environment, learning becomes like the air—it's in and around us.